The Journey from Artifi...
Convolutional Neural Network

The Journey from Artificial to Convolutional Neural Network

Amit Verma

CWP

Central West Publishing

Disclaimer
Every effort has been made by the publisher, editors and authors while preparing this book, however, no warranties are made regarding the accuracy and completeness of the content. The publisher, editors and authors disclaim without any limitation all warranties as well as any implied warranties about sales, along with fitness of the content for a particular purpose. Citation of any website and other information sources does not mean any endorsement from the publisher, editors and authors. For ascertaining the suitability of the contents contained herein for a particular lab or commercial use, consultation with the subject expert is needed. In addition, while using the information and methods contained herein, the practitioners and researchers need to be mindful for their own safety, along with the safety of others, including the professional parties and premises for whom they have professional responsibility. To the fullest extent of law, the publisher, editors and authors are not liable in all circumstances (special, incidental, and consequential) for any injury and/or damage to persons and property, along with any potential loss of profit and other commercial damages due to the use of any methods, products, guidelines, procedures contained in the material herein.

A catalogue record for this book is available from the National Library of Australia

NATIONAL LIBRARY OF AUSTRALIA

ISBN (print): 978-1-922617-42-2

Preface

Dr. Geoffrey Hinton is considered as father of Artificial Neural Network (ANN) and Deep leaning. ANN is a powerful technology that has brought a revolutionary change in the digital world. Today ANN is being used in every field. It has created a huge requirement of employments in various industries such as software, agriculture, medical, construction, aeronautical, and many more. ANN has opened up many areas for researchers. Currently, researchers are utilizing ANN excellently in many different fields mostly in medicine and agriculture related areas. In ANN, models are trained using various features extracted from previously collected data to predict the results over unknown data.

However, extraction of features from the available dataset requires good domain knowledge. Deep learning has solved this constraint by automating the process of feature extraction. Deep learning based Convolutional Neural Network (CNN) has automated the process of feature extraction without any human intervention. These extracted features are further passed as input to ANN for training of the model. Dr. Yann LeCun has given this remarkable update in the field of neural network which make the process of model training more powerful and easy especially in image classification. Inspired by such a huge contribution of AI in digitization, many institutes have adopted AI/ML as a separate course instead of a subject in Computer Science and Engineering. Almost every company in today's date is adopting AI very fast, due to which the demand for AI / ML engineering and data scientists in the market has increased rapidly. ANN and CNN are now inseparable parts of AI/ML and considered as the basic building blocks to design any ML network.

Table of Contents

1

Concepts of Numpy and Pandas

Before moving to the theoretical and practical implementation of any neural network model, it is very much required to have knowledge about some basic and important concepts of Numpy and Pandas. Therefore, in this chapter we will discuss about some concepts of Numpy and Padas that you will find very useful in the practical implementation of any neural network and dealing with datasets. Numpy and Pandas play a pivotal role in pre-processing of data and loading data for training and testing of the model.

1.1 Numpy

Numpy is a library having wide range of inbuilt function provided by python to deal with single or multi-dimensional arrays. Numpy arrays are much faster than the traditional python lists and take very less amount of memory as compared to list as shown in Example 1.

```python
import sys
a = [1, 2, 3, 4]
print(sys.getsizeof(a))
```

104

```python
import numpy as np
b = np.array([1, 2, 3, 4])
print(b.size)
```

4

Example 1. Numpy array take much less memory as compared to list.

Numpy array provide many useful built in attributes, which help in dealing with big dataset that is the primary step of any neural network model. Here is the list of some advantageous attributes with examples.

1.1.1 array() and ndim() - Numpy facilitate you for creating arrays of multiple dimensions using the array() function. In the below examples from Example 2 to Example 5 we have created array from dimension 0 to 3. Moreover, used ndim function to check the dimension of each array. The ndim() is among important attributes used in implementation of any neural network based model.

```python
import numpy as np
a0 = np.array(0)
print(f'value = {a0}')
print(f'dimension = {a0.ndim}')


value = 0
dimension = 0
```

Example 2. Numpy array of 0 dimension.

We can also check the dimension of an array by passing name of an array as a parameter in ndim function as shown in Example 3.

```python
a1 = np.array([1,2])
print(f'value = {a1}')
print(f'dimension = {a1.ndim}')
print(f'dimension = {np.ndim(a1)}')


value = [1 2]
dimension = 1
dimension = 1
```

Example 3. Numpy array of 1 dimension.

```
a2 = np.array([[1,2],[3,4]])
print(f'value = {a2}')
print(f'dimension = {a2.ndim}')

value = [[1 2]
 [3 4]]
dimension = 2
```

Example 4. Numpy array of 2 dimension.

```
a3 = np.array([[[1,2],[3,4]],[[5,6],[7,8]]])
print(f'value = {a3}')
print(f'dimension = {a3.ndim}')

value = [[[1 2]
  [3 4]]

 [[5 6]
  [7 8]]]
dimension = 3
```

Example 5. Numpy array of 3 dimension.

1.1.2 shape – The shape attribute allow you to check the number of elements in each dimension, it return the tuple with appropriate information about the numpy array. Considering an Example 6 shown below to check the shape of 2D Numpy array.

```
a2 = np.array([[1,2],[3,4]])
print(f'shape = {a2.shape}')
```

```
shape = (2, 2)
```

Example 6. Showing the number of element in each dimension that is Row and Column (2x2)

Example 6 showing (2, 2) elements in row and column of 2D array which seem to be obvious as we have created the array and we already know about the dimension of the array. However, this attribute play very important role when we are not aware about the dataset. For instance if we have to train our model using some unknown dataset D1. Let D1 is having large number of images of same size then using shape attribute we can check the number of images and dimension of each image present in D1. If D1 is having 10000 images and each image of dimension 28x28, after loading data in some variable say dataset. Then dataset.shape will print tuple (10000, 28, 28) representing the number of images and dimension of each image as well. For better understanding let's take more practical example. Considering well-known MNIST dataset ("https://storage.googleapis.com/tensorflow/tf-keras-datasets/") which is having a large number of images of numeric data (0 to 9) and we want to check the number and dimension of images. In Example 7, shape attribute provide us the information about the number of images and dimension of each image use for training purpose.

```
In [1]: import tensorflow as tf
        from keras.preprocessing.image import ImageDataGenerator
        from keras.datasets import mnist

In [2]: (trainX, trainY) , (testX, testY) = mnist.load_data()

In [3]: print(trainX.shape)

        (60000, 28, 28)
```

Example 7. Detail about the Training data from MNIST dataset.

1.1.3 reshape – The reshape attribute use to provide new shape to existing array, here shape is the information about the number of element in each dimension of an array. The reshape attribute is also one of the easy and powerful function of numpy library, which is very useful in implementing almost every neural network model. For better understanding of this function, we are including couple of examples. In Example 8, one dimension array a1 reshaped in 2D array. However, during reshaping any numpy array we should mind that new shape of an array should appropriately match the number of elements in an array. For example, if a1 is any numpy array of 9 elements and we try to reshape a1 in 3x2 dimension than the interpreter will show exception (error) as shown in Example 9.

```python
import numpy as np
a1 = np.array([1,2,3,4,5,6,7,8,9])
print(f'dimension = {a1.ndim}')
print(a1)
a1 = a1.reshape(3,3)
print(f'new dimension = {a1.ndim}')
print(a1)

dimension = 1
[1 2 3 4 5 6 7 8 9]
new dimension = 2
[[1 2 3]
 [4 5 6]
 [7 8 9]]
```

Example 8. Reshaping 1D array into 2D array.

```
import numpy as np
```

```
a1 = np.array([1,2,3,4,5,6,7,8,9])
print(f'dimension = {a1.ndim}')
print(a1)
a1 = a1.reshape(3,2)
print(f'new dimension = {a1.ndim}')
print(a1)
```

```
dimension = 1
[1 2 3 4 5 6 7 8 9]
```

```
-------------------------------------------------------------------------
ValueError                                Traceback (most recent call last)
<ipython-input-5-14aaaa4e6347> in <module>
      2 print(f'dimension = {a1.ndim}')
      3 print(a1)
----> 4 a1 = a1.reshape(3,2)
      5 print(f'new dimension = {a1.ndim}')
      6 print(a1)

ValueError: cannot reshape array of size 9 into shape (3,2)
```

Example 9. Cannot reshape an array with unsuitable dimension.

The reshape attribute is also very useful in implementing neural network models, as it is very important to provide complete information about the dataset to the model for training. As we have seen in Example 7, trainX.shape provide information about the training data that it will be having 60000 images and each image is of dimension 28x28. However, before using this data to train the model it is also required to provide information about the value of each pixel. That is, we should provide the information that whether the images are color images (with RGB channels) or grey-scale images (single channel). In case of color images, each pixel of an image have three different values where as in case of grey-scale images each pixels of an image have single value. Therefore, before proving MNIST training data, we have to reshape the data to provide complete information to the model as shown in Example 10. As we have seen in Example 7, trainX.shape is (60000, 28, 28). Therefore in Example 10 trainX.shape[0] is 60000 which is the total number of images in training dataset. Here we have increase the existing dimension of trainX by adding one more dimension which is providing the information that each pixel of image is having single value. That is all images in trainX data are grey scale images. Now if we check the dimension of trainX then it will be 4 instead of 3 as shown in below Example 11.

```
trainX = trainX.reshape((trainX.shape[0], 28, 28, 1))
```

```
print(trainX.shape)
```

```
(60000, 28, 28, 1)
```

Example 10. Reshape the dataset.

```
trainX = trainX.reshape((trainX.shape[0], 28, 28, 1))
testX = testX.reshape((testX.shape[0], 28, 28, 1))
```

```
print(trainX.shape)
print(trainX.ndim)
```

```
(60000, 28, 28, 1)
4
```

Example 11. New dimension of trainX dataset.

1.1.4 dtype – The dtype attribute is use to check the type of an array (Example 12) as in many cases it is very much require to know the type of elements in numpy array to perform certain operations.

```
a1 = np.array([1,2,3,4,5,6,7,8,9])
print(a1.dtype)
```

```
int32
```

Example 12. Showing the data-type of elements of numpy array.

This dtype attribute is very important attribute in implementing the deep learning or any neural network model. Before training any model we have to perform pre-processing of data, therefore it is very much required to check the type of data for performing appropriate operation. Like, if we want to normalize all the pixel values of any grey-scale image between 0 and 1. Then we have to perform the division operation (divide each pixel by 255) over image pixels. However, before that it would be require to check the type of pixel values and to change the data type to float (if required). Same procedure followed with MNIST training data also as shown in below Example 13.

```python
print(trainX.dtype)
```

```
uint8
```

```python
# convert from integers to floats (NORMALIZATION)
trainX = trainX.astype('float32')
print(trainX.dtype)
# normalize to range 0-1
trainX = trainX / 255.0
```

```
float32
```

Example 13. Use of dtype in normalization of data.

1.1.6. Slicing of Numpy Array - Slicing is an important concept that we should know and have good command over it before getting to implementation of any neural network based model. This topic play pivotal role in almost every deep learning model. Therefore, in this topic we will discuss multiple examples related to slicing of numpy array. We will start with elementary examples and discuss some good examples later. The dictionary meaning of slice is part of something. So, in context of numpy array slice mean part of array. Before that, we should know the indexing of an array in python. In python array is index from 0 to n-1, where n is the number of items in an array. Index 0 is representing the very first element and n-1 representing the last element. In python, array indexing can be done from the last element also in which the last element is represented by -1, and proceed towards the first element in decrementing order as shown in Fig 1.1. For better understanding let's see an example related to array index (Example 14).

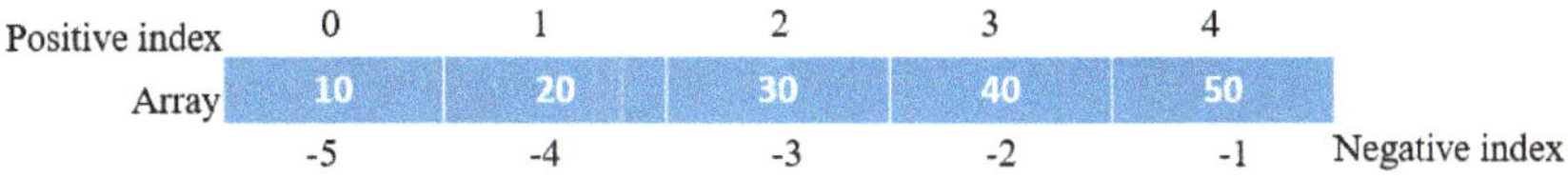

Positive index	0	1	2	3	4	
Array	10	20	30	40	50	
	-5	-4	-3	-2	-1	Negative index

Fig. 1.1 Indexing of array

```
a1= np.array([10, 20, 30, 40 , 50])
print(f'first element (left most element) at index 0 = {a1[0]}')
print(f'last element at index 4 = {a1[4]}')
print(f'first element at index -5 = {a1[-5]}')
print(f'last element (right most element) at index -1 = {a1[-1]}')

first element (left most element) at index 0 = 10
last element at index 4 = 50
first element at index -5 = 10
last element (right most element) at index -1 = 50
```

Example 14. Indexing of Array.

Now we will see the concept of slicing in numpy arrays, the syntax of slicing is **[start : end]** or **[start : end : step]** in which start and end represent the indexes and step represent the gap between the indexes. Step is optional, that is the absence of step will be considered as 1. However, we should keep in mind that in slicing, index of end position get excluded so we always take end index one position ahead than the required one. As shown in Example 15 in which line 2 is printing whole array. Where start is represented by index 0, end by index 6 (one more than last index of a1 that is 5) and step represented by 1. If we skip start index in slicing array than 0 is considered as default value as shown in line 3. Similarly, the default value for the end is total number of elements in an array or one more than the last array index (5 in this case) and 1 for steps. That is why with the execution of the last four lines of the below example still we are getting output as a whole array. In the last line of the example the absence of step will consider its default value that is 1 and print all the value of array a1.

```
a1= np.array([10, 20, 30, 40 , 50, 60])
print(a1[0:6:1])#[start : end : step]
print(a1[:6:1])
print(a1[::1])
print(a1[::])
print(a1[:])
```

```
[10 20 30 40 50 60]
[10 20 30 40 50 60]
[10 20 30 40 50 60]
[10 20 30 40 50 60]
[10 20 30 40 50 60]
```

Example 15. Slicing of Numpy array.

Now consider the variation in outputs by changing the slicing indexes and step values. In Example 16, a1[1 : 4] will print the elements from index 1 to index 3 (one less than end = 4) one after another as step is missing in slicing so one would be considered as default step value. However, a1[1 : 4 : 2] will print the alternate values from index 1 to index 3 as the step value is 2 in this case.

```
a1= np.array([10, 20, 30, 40 , 50, 60])
print(a1[1:4])#start = 1, end = 4 and step = default value(that is 1)
print(a1[1:4:2])# start = 1, end = 4 and step = 2
```

```
[20 30 40]
[20 40]
```

Example 16. Slicing with step = 2

It is also possible to print the reverse array using slicing without us-ing any loop, just by changing the values of slicing indexes and steps. Considering Example 17, in which we have printed first five values in reverse order. In line 2, a1[4 : : -1] as step = -1 it means we proceed in reverse order with start = 4 to end = total number of elements in array (default value of end). And in line 3, a1[4 : -7 : -1] end = -7 as the last index is -6 according to reverse indexing as shown in Fig. 1.1. Therefore, all the elements from index 4 to very first element will print in reverse order. Similarly, in last line, a1[-2 : -7 : -1] all elements will be presented according to the reverse array indexing.

```
a1 = np.array([10,20,30,40,50,60])
print(a1[4 : : -1])
print(a1[4 : -7 : -1])
print(a1[-2 : -7 : -1])
```

```
[50 40 30 20 10]
[50 40 30 20 10]
[50 40 30 20 10]
```

Example 17. Printing numpy array in reverse order with slicing.

Now we will consider the examples with slicing in 2D array. The 2D array can also be considered as two 1D arrays. As shown in Example 18, Array a1 is of size 2x5 which means that a1 is 2D array with two rows and five columns as shown in Fig 1.2. During slicing the value before comma represents the number of rows and after comma represents number of columns.

	Column 0	Column 1	Column 2	Column 3	Column 4
Row 0	1	2	3	4	5
Row 1	6	7	8	9	10

Fig. 1.2 Block representation of 2D array a1 (as mention in Example 18).

We can apply slicing in each dimension (number of rows and number of column in this case) of array a1. In line 1 of Example 18, a1[0 , 0] means value at 0th row and 0th column therefore, a1[0 , 0] = 1. In line 3, a1[0 , :] means 0th row and all columns so, all value of 0th row will be get printed that is [1, 2, 3, 4, 5]. Similarly, line 4 a1[1 , :] means 1st row and all columns therefore, values of all column of row 1 will be get printed that is [6, 7, 8, 9, 10]. In line 5, a1[: , 0] means all rows and 0th column which mean that all values of 0th column will be get printed that is [1, 6]. Similarly, in line 6 a1[: , 1] all rows are selected and column 1 is selected so all values of column 1 will be get printed that is

[2 , 7]. Finally, in last line a1[: , :] all rows and all columns are selected therefore, whole array will be get printed on the console screen.

```
a1 = np.array([[1, 2, 3, 4, 5], [6, 7, 8, 9, 10]])
print(a1[0,0])#element of 0th row and 0th column
print(a1[0,:])#all elements of 0th row
print(a1[1,:])#all elements of 1st row
print(a1[:,0])#0th elements of each row
print(a1[:,1])#1st elements of each row
print(a1[:,:])#all elements of each row
```

```
1
[1 2 3 4 5]
[ 6  7  8  9 10]
[1 6]
[2 7]
[[ 1  2  3  4  5]
 [ 6  7  8  9 10]]
```

Example 18. Slicing 2D (2x5) array.

Now considering a 2D array a1 of bigger dimension that is 4x5 as represented in Fig. 1. 3. In which first dimension represents the number of rows from index 0 to 3 and second dimension represent number of columns from index 0 to 4. In below Example 19, slicing applied on 2D array a1.

	Column 0	Column 1	Column 2	Column 3	Column 4
Row 0	1	2	3	4	5
Row 1	6	7	8	9	10
Row 2	11	12	13	14	15
Row 3	16	17	18	19	20

Fig. 1.3 Block diagram of 2D array a1 (as mention in Example 18).

In line 2 of Example 19, a1[0:1 , 0:1] means start = 0 and end = 1 for first dimension (number of rows) and start = 0 and end = 1 for second dimension (number of columns). Excluding end positions from both dimensions, 0th row and 0th column will be selected to give [[1]] as output of line 2. In line 3, a1[0:2 , 0:5] means row 0 and row 1 are selected similarly after excluding index 2. Similarly, excluding index 5 from second dimension column 0 to column 4 will be selected. Therefore, execution of line 3 print all column values of row 0 and 1. In line 4, a1[0:4 , 0:5:2] as per first dimension that is (0:4) row 0 to row 3 are selected. Moreover, according to second dimension (0:5:2) all alternating columns that is 0, 2, 4 are selected. Similarly, in line 5 that is a1[0:4:2 , 0:5:2] all alternate rows (0, 2) and all alternate columns (0, 2, 4) are selected in first and second dimension respectively. Last line 6 is identical to line number 5, will produce similar output.

```
a1 = np.array([[1, 2, 3, 4, 5],
               [6, 7, 8, 9, 10],
               [11, 12, 13, 14, 15],
               [16, 17, 18, 19, 20]])
print(a1[0:1 , 0:1])
print(a1[0:2 , 0:5])
print(a1[0:4 , 0:5:2])
print(a1[0:4:2 , 0:5:2])
print(a1[: :2 , : :2])
```

```
[[1]]
[[ 1  2  3  4  5]
 [ 6  7  8  9 10]]
[[ 1  3  5]
 [ 6  8 10]
 [11 13 15]
 [16 18 20]]
[[ 1  3  5]
 [11 13 15]]
[[ 1  3  5]
 [11 13 15]]
```

Example 19. Slicing 2D (4x5) array.

1.2 Pandas

Pandas is another very important python library, which provide very powerful attributes to deal with large datasets. For understanding and implementing any neural network, datasets are mandatory part. Therefore, in this section we will study some basic and important concepts of pandas. Pandas library mainly deal with the labeled data, provide various operations to manipulate data. Here we discuss some major attributes of pandas that will be very useful in implementing deep learning based models.

1.2.1 Pandas Dataframe - Dataframe is a 2D mutable and heterogeneous data structure representing labeled rows and columns. In simple words, dataframe is like a table with multiple rows and columns having different values. Each row in table represented with indexes from 0 to n-1 (n is the total number of rows) whereas each column having column name which could be any user-define name. Dataframes are widely used to deal with datasets. A simple dataframe shown in Fig. 1.4 having four labeled (user-defined) columns and four indexed rows from 0 to 3.

		Name	Age	Roll Number	Course
	0	Aman	20	20012	Fine Arts
	1	John	21	20032	Science
	2	Rita	22	20034	Engineering
	3	Suman	19	20045	Commerce

Rows indexes 0 to 3

Fig. 1.4 Dataframe representing record of four students.

Dataframes are created to load data in a variable from already existing data in excel file (.csv file) stored in hard disc. By loading data in a variable we can easily perform multiple operation on data and analyze the changes without effecting the original data in excel file. To better understand this powerful concept of dataframe, lets take a simple example in which a dictionary is converted into dataframe as shown in Example 20. In the below example, dictionary containing record of a student is stored in a dataframe df, which convert the dictionary into 2D (row, column) tabular data structure.

```
import pandas as pd
```

```
data = {
    "Name": "Aman",
    "Age": [20],
    "Roll Number": [200012],
    "Course": "Fine Arts"
}
df = pd.DataFrame(data)
print(df)
```

```
     Name   Age   Roll Number        Course
0    Aman    20        200012     Fine Arts
```

Example 20. Converting dictionary with record of a student into dataframe.

Another example (Example 21), converting dictionary with multiple records into a dataframe df. Dictionary keys are converted into column label (column name) and associated list as column values.

```
data = {
    "Name": ["Aman", "John", "Rita", "Sakshi"],
    "Age": [20, 21, 21, 20],
    "Roll Number": [200012, 200033, 200042, 200055],
    "Course": ["Fine Arts", "Engineering", "Engineeing", "Fine Arts"]
}
df = pd.DataFrame(data)
print(df)
```

```
      Name   Age   Roll Number        Course
0     Aman    20        200012     Fine Arts
1     John    21        200033   Engineering
2     Rita    21        200042    Engineeing
3   Sakshi    20        200055     Fine Arts
```

Example 21. Converting dictionary with multiple records into dataframe.

Loading data into datafarme is meaningless if we don't able to access the data for manipulation. Therefore, two important attributes are provided by pandas library to access the data from dataframe. The .loc and .iloc are two pandas attributes used for accessing data from dataframe.

1.2.2 loc – The .loc is used for retrieving and updating data from dataframe. It is not a method so we always use square bracket instead of round bracket with .loc. Moreover, takes two inputs that is row label and column label (optional). It requires at least one input that is row index, else it will show an error (Example 22). In Example 22, 0 to 3 are row label and Name, Age, Roll Number, and Course are column label.

```python
import pandas as pd
```

```python
data = {
    "Name":["Aman", "John", "Rita", "Sakshi"],
    "Age":[20,21,21,20],
    "Roll Number":[200012, 200033, 200042, 200055],
    "Course":["Fine Arts", "Engineering", "Engineering", "Fine Arts"]
}
df1 = pd.DataFrame(data)
print(df1)
```

```
     Name  Age  Roll Number       Course
0    Aman   20       200012    Fine Arts
1    John   21       200033  Engineering
2    Rita   21       200042  Engineering
3  Sakshi   20       200055    Fine Arts
```

```python
df1.loc[]
```

```
  File "<ipython-input-45-8e963487e0cd>", line 1
    df1.loc[]
            ^
SyntaxError: invalid syntax
```

Example 22. .loc cannot be empty, requiring at least one input that is row label.

Row label is mandatory in .loc to access the data of particular row as shown in Example 23. Here 0 is the row label to access all the data associated with that row label.

```
import pandas as pd
```

```
data = {
    "Name":["Aman", "John", "Rita", "Sakshi"],
    "Age":[20,21,21,20],
    "Roll Number":[200012, 200033, 200042, 200055],
    "Course":["Fine Arts", "Engineering", "Engineering", "Fine Arts"]
}
df1 = pd.DataFrame(data)
print(df1)
```

```
    Name  Age  Roll Number        Course
0   Aman   20       200012     Fine Arts
1   John   21       200033   Engineering
2   Rita   21       200042   Engineering
3 Sakshi   20       200055     Fine Arts
```

```
df1.loc[0]
```

```
Name                Aman
Age                   20
Roll Number       200012
Course         Fine Arts
Name: 0, dtype: object
```

Example 23. Access data of row 0.

We cannot mention column label as only input in .loc as shown in below Example 24. The .loc attribute require two inputs that is row and column label. In which row label is a mandatory input. That means if we try to access the data using only column label and without row label then the program will give error as shown in below example. In which by writing a statement df1.loc['Name'] we are trying to access all the data under the column label 'Name'. However, as column label cannot be used as only parameter in .loc to access the data therefore program is giving error. The error is rectified in upcoming examples.

```python
import pandas as pd
```

```python
data = {
    "Name":["Aman", "John", "Rita", "Sakshi"],
    "Age":[20,21,21,20],
    "Roll Number":[200012, 200033, 200042, 200055],
    "Course":["Fine Arts", "Engineering", "Engineering", "Fine Arts"]
}
df1 = pd.DataFrame(data)
print(df1)
```

```
     Name  Age  Roll Number       Course
0    Aman   20       200012    Fine Arts
1    John   21       200033  Engineering
2    Rita   21       200042  Engineering
3  Sakshi   20       200055    Fine Arts
```

```python
df1.loc["Name"]
```

```
-------------------------------------------------------------------
KeyError                            Traceback (most recent call last)
<ipython-input-47-12113077e45c> in <module>
----> 1 df1.loc["Name"]
```

Example 24. Column label cannot be used as only input with .loc

For accessing particular value from the dataframe we have to mention the location of the value according to row and column label. To access name "John" we can write

 df1.loc[1, "Name"]

where '1' is the row label and 'Name' is column label. Further to access all the values of particular column "Age" we can write

df1.loc[:, "Age"]

where colon(:) means all the rows of column 'Age'.

In .loc we can not access the data using column default indexes like 1 instead of 'Age' it will give error as shown in below Example 25. Therefore, in .loc we should know the column names beforehand. In Example 25 we have consider dataframe df1 as mention in above examples.

```
df1.loc[:, "Age"]
```

```
0    20
1    21
2    21
3    20
Name: Age, dtype: int64
```

```
df1.loc[:, 1]
```

```
-------------------------------------------------------------------------
KeyError                                    Traceback (most recent call last)
~\Anaconda3\lib\site-packages\pandas\core\indexes\base.py in get_loc(self, |
   3079                 try:
-> 3080                     return self._engine.get_loc(casted_key)
   3081                 except KeyError as err:
```

Example 25. Index cannot be used with .loc.

Data can also be updated using .loc as shown in Example 26 (data-frame df1), where first value of column 'Name' is update to 'Amit' from 'Aman'. All values of particular columns can also be updated using .loc (Example 27).

```
df1.loc[0, 'Name'] = "Amit"
```

```
print(df1)
```

```
        Name  Age  Roll Number        Course
0       Amit   20       200012     Fine Arts
1       John   21       200033   Engineering
2       Rita   21       200042   Engineering
3     Sakshi   20       200055     Fine Arts
```

Example 26. Updated the first name of datafram that is Aman to Amit.

```
df1.loc[:, 'Name'] = "Amit"
```

```
print(df1)
```

```
    Name  Age  Roll Number        Course
0   Amit   20       200012     Fine Arts
1   Amit   21       200033   Engineering
2   Amit   21       200042   Engineering
3   Amit   20       200055     Fine Arts
```

Example 27. All values of column 'Name' has been updated to 'Amit'.

1.2.3. iloc – The .iloc attribute of pandas use to access and update the data in dataframe through row and column indexes. In case of .iloc we don't need to know about the labels of the dataset before using it. However, in .loc we have to know about the labels of dataset to access the data. As mention in Example 25, where we get error when we try to access all data under 'Age' column using index with the statement df1.loc[:, 1]. However by replacing .loc with .iloc we can access all the data under column 'Age' using index 1 instead of column label.
We can also access single value from the dataframe such as 'Amit' of column 'Name' with .iloc by specifying the indexes as shown in below line of code.

print(df1.iloc[1,0])

Where 1 and 0 represent the row and column index respectively.
Similarly, we can update any value in the dataframe using .iloc as shown below Example 28 in which first value of column 'Name' that is 'Aman' at index [0, 0] is changed to 'Ankit'.

```python
import pandas as pd
```

```python
data = {
    "Name":["Aman", "John", "Rita", "Sakshi"],
    "Age":[20,21,21,20],
    "Roll Number":[200012, 200033, 200042, 200055],
    "Course":["Fine Arts", "Engineering", "Engineering", "Fine Arts"]
}
df1 = pd.DataFrame(data)
print(df1)
```

```
     Name  Age  Roll Number       Course
0    Aman   20       200012    Fine Arts
1    John   21       200033  Engineering
2    Rita   21       200042  Engineering
3  Sakshi   20       200055    Fine Arts
```

```python
df1.iloc[0,0] = "Anikit"
```

```python
print(df1)
```

```
     Name  Age  Roll Number       Course
0  Anikit   20       200012    Fine Arts
1    John   21       200033  Engineering
2    Rita   21       200042  Engineering
3  Sakshi   20       200055    Fine Arts
```

Example 28. Aman is updated as Anikit.

Summary

Numpy is a python library use to deal with arrays. The array and ndim functions of numpy used to create arrays and for checking the dimension of the array. The shape attribute of numpy return tuple with number of elements in each dimension of numpy array. Further, reshape function is used for changing the dimension of an array without chaining the content. The dtype object return the data type of the numpy array. Slicing of numpy array use to extract portion of an array from some starting to ending index. Numpy arrays are indexed in both direction that is in forward and backward. In forward, from 0 to n-1 and from -1 to -n in backward direction where n represents the total number of elements in an array.

Pandas is python library, which provides multiple attributes to analyze and manipulate large labeled datasets. Pandas dataframe is row and column (tabular) representation of the dataset. In dataframes,

.loc and .iloc functions used for accessing and updating the data. In .loc data from dataframe can be accessed using labels whereas in .iloc data can be accessed using indexes instead of labels. Therefore, in .iloc it is not required to know the labels of the dataset before-hand.

Exercise

Solution provided for questions with asterisk symbol (*).

1. *Write a program (WAP) in python to create numpy array, having number from 1 to 5 and increment 2 in each element of a1 without using any loop.
2. *WAP in python to create numpy array with first 15 natural numbers and find the occurrence of 4 in the array.
3. WAP in python to create numpy array with any 10 user define integer numbers and find all the occurrences of an integer number input by the user.
4. *WAP in python to create two 1D numpy arrays of 9 integer numbers in each array. Reshape both the arrays in 2D arrays of size 3x3 and add both the arrays.
5. *WAP in python to create a numpy array and check the data type of elements in the array. Further, rescale all the elements within the range of 0 to 1.
6. WAP in python to create a numpy array and print the elements of an array in reverse order without loop.
7. *WAP in python to flat a user defined 2D numpy array. Moreover, display the before and after shape of numpy array.
8. Explain the importance of dataframe in pandas with the help of program in python.
9. Explain the difference between .loc and .iloc. Also, write a program in python to support the answer.
10. *WAP in python to create a dictionary to maintain the record of 6 students with labels as 'name', 'rollno', 'age', and 'course'. Convert the dictionary into dataframe and print all the students with the same age.

Solutions:

Question 1.

```python
import numpy as np
```

```python
a1 = np.array([1, 2, 3, 4])
a1 = a1+2
print(a1)
```

```
[3 4 5 6]
```

Question 2.

```python
a1 = np.arange(15)
print(a1)
print(np.where(a1 == 4))
```

```
[ 0  1  2  3  4  5  6  7  8  9 10 11 12 13 14]
(array([4], dtype=int64),)
```

Question 4.

```python
a1 = np.array([2, 3, 4, 5, 6, 7, 3, 4, 6])
a2 = np.array([1, 32, 43, 5, 65, 7, 37, 49, 6])
```

```python
a1 = a1.reshape(3,3)
a2 = a2.reshape(3,3)
```

```python
result = np.add(a1, a2)
print(result)
```

```
[[ 3 35 47]
 [10 71 14]
 [40 53 12]]
```

Question 5.

```
a1 = np.array([2, 3, 4, 5, 6, 1, 2, 3])
print(a1.dtype)
a1_f = a1.astype('float32')
norm_a1 = (a1_f - np.min(a1_f))/(np.max(a1_f) - np.min(a1_f))
print(a1_f.dtype)
```

```
int32
float32
```

Question 7.

```
a1 = np.array([[2, 3, 4],
               [5, 6, 7]])
print(a1)
print(f'Actual shape of array a1 = {a1.shape}')
a1_flat = a1.flatten()
print(a1_flat)
print(f'Shape of array a1 after flattening = {a1_flat.shape}')
```

```
[[2 3 4]
 [5 6 7]]
Actual shape of array a1 = (2, 3)
[2 3 4 5 6 7]
Shape of array a1 after flattening = (6,)
```

Question 10.

```
import pandas as pd
```

```
data = {
    "Name":["Aman", "John", "Rita", "Sakshi"],
    "Age":[20,21,22,20],
    "Roll Number":[200012, 200033, 200042, 200055],
    "Course":["Fine Arts", "Engineering", "Engineering", "Fine Arts"]
}
df1 = pd.DataFrame(data)
print(df1)
print(df1[df1.duplicated('Age', keep=False)])
```

```
     Name  Age  Roll Number       Course
0    Aman   20       200012    Fine Arts
1    John   21       200033  Engineering
2    Rita   22       200042  Engineering
3  Sakshi   20       200055    Fine Arts
     Name  Age  Roll Number     Course
0    Aman   20       200012  Fine Arts
3  Sakshi   20       200055  Fine Arts
```

2

Introduction to Artificial Neural Network

An artificial neural network is a computational model, a mimic of the structure of actual brain. Majorly use in classification and object detection process. In this chapter, we have discussed the basic structure of ANN and its learning process with example.

2.1 Artificial Neural Network

ANN is collection of connected neurons (nodes) in various layers. Each layer receive the input from the previous layer and pass output to the next layer. ANN have two compulsory layers that is input and output layer. Input and output layers can have multiple hidden layers in between. Neurons in different layers remain connected with edges, each edge have some weight (any real number). These weights are adjusted to decide the contribution of particular neuron in the output. ANN based model is motivated from the actual brain structure. As in actual brain, dendrites receive input that processed by the nucleus and pass to the axons terminals through axons. Similarly, in ANN dendrites act as input layer, nucleus play a role of neurons, axons as weighted edges, and axon terminals act as output layer. The typical architecture of an actual brain and artificial neural network shown in Fig. 2.1.

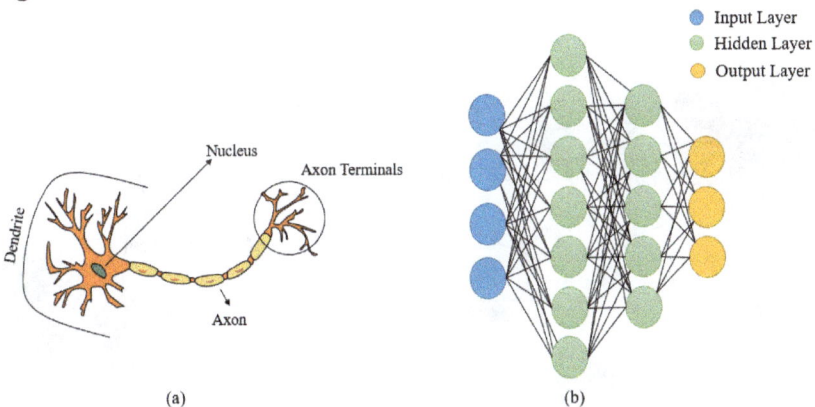

Fig. 2.1 (a) Brain neuron structure (b) ANN basic structure.

2.2 Learning Process of Neural Network

To understand the basic structure of a neural network, let us consider a very simple network as shown in Fig. 2.2. The network is having input layer with bias node, single neuron in the hidden layer, and an output layer. The neuron calculate z and pass it to activation function $f(z)$ to calculate φ, using Eq. 1 and 2. The calculated values passed to the output or another hidden layer (if any). Activation functions discussed in detail in chapter 6.

$$z = \sum_{i=1}^{n} (w_i * x_i) + w_b * b \qquad (1)$$

$$\varphi = f(z) \qquad (2)$$

The output y' is the predicted or hypothetical value according to the particular inputs. This predicted value y' compared with the actual value or ground truth y for the particular set of input values. The ground truth for all input values were already remain mentioned in the dataset that is used to train the neural network. The difference between the ground truth y (dependent variable) and predicted value y' is called cost C or Mean Squared Error (MSE) represented by Eq. 3.

$$C = \frac{1}{2}(y' - y)^2 \qquad (3)$$

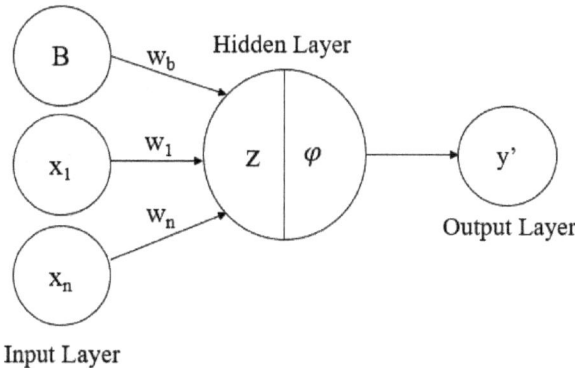

Fig. 2.2. Simple neural network with bias node in input layer and one node in hidden layer.

If the value of C is higher than the weights are adjusted to recalculate the predicted value y' this process of adjusting weights called as back propagation. Now again we calculate the value of C based on ground truth y and the predicted value y'. This process continues until C get minimized. Considering one example to train a simple neural network for implementing AND logical gate. That means, if the neural network receives two ones than only the output will be one else in all cases the output would be zero as shown in the table 1. There are two input variables x1 and x2 and corresponding ground truth y. Now we will train the neural network using the dataset.

Table 1. AND operation

x1	x2	y
0	0	0
0	1	0
1	0	0
1	1	1

As the dataset having two input variables therefore, input layer will have two nodes for input and one bias node. Input to bias node can be any real number for example +1. Assuming single node in the hidden layer. Further, as the output can be either 0 or 1 therefore, output layer can have single node. Now let us consider some random real numbers as the initial weights w_b, w_1 and w_2 as shown in Fig. 2.3.

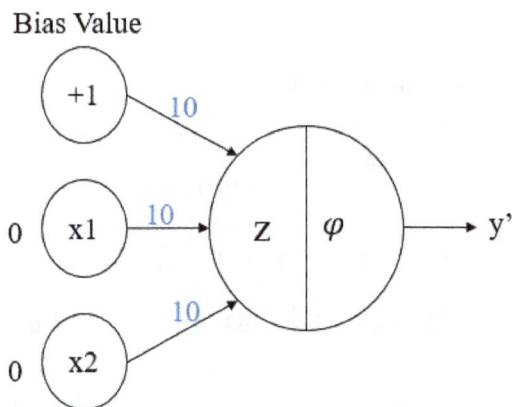

Fig. 2.3 Initial weights are assigned to the neural network to predict output for input x1 = 0 and x2 = 0.

Following are the steps involved in training a neural network for implementing AND gate.

Step 1. Assign some real numbers as initial weights (10 in this case) to the neural network.

Step 2. Calculate z using Eq. 1.

$$z = 1 * 10 + 0 * 10 + 0 * 10$$

$$z = 10$$

Step 3. Value of z assigned to activation function to calculate φ using Eq. 2. Let us consider threshold activation function in this case as shown in Fig. 2.4. Threshold activation function return 1 for all positive values of z else return 0.

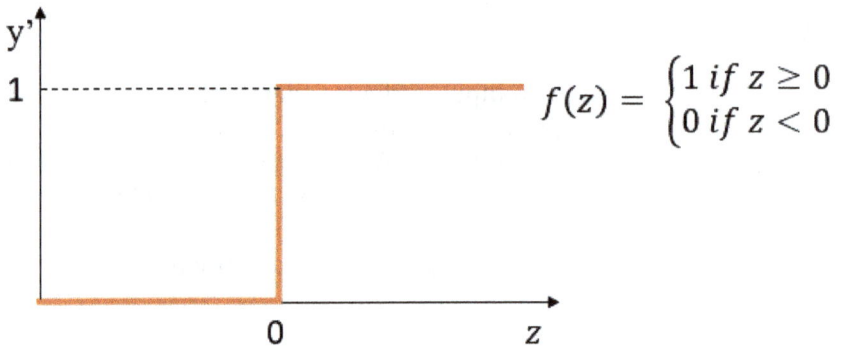

$$f(z) = \begin{cases} 1 \ if \ z \geq 0 \\ 0 \ if \ z < 0 \end{cases}$$

Fig. 2.4 Threshold activation function.

Therefore,

$$\varphi = f(10)$$

$$\varphi = 1$$

The value of φ will be passed to the output layer as predicted value y'.

Step 4. Now we calculate mean squared error using Eq. 3 by replacing the values of y' = 1 (predicted value) and y = 0 (ground truth) as mention in the table 1.

$$C = \frac{1}{2}(1 - 0)^2$$

$$C = \frac{1}{2}$$

As the calculated cost or MSE is very high therefore, we adjust the weights using back propagation and repeat rest of the steps.
Let us assign some other weights to the neural network as shown in the Fig. 2.5.

Step 1. This time we consider -20 for bias value and 10, 10 for other two input values.

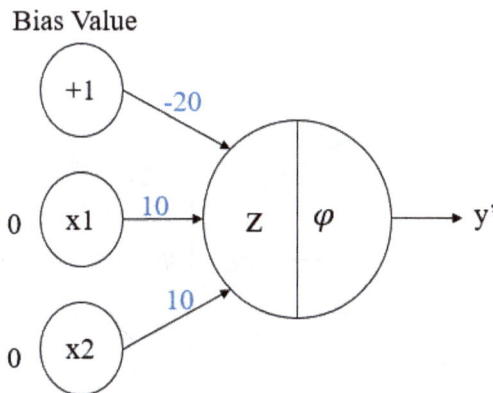

Fig. 2.5 New weights are assigned to the neural network to predict output for input x1 = 0 and x2 = 0.

Step 2. Calculate z using Eq. 1.

$$z = 1 * (-20) + 0 * 10 + 0 * 10$$

$$z = -20$$

Step 3. Calculate the value of z using threshold activation function. Therefore,

$$\varphi = f(-20)$$

$$\varphi = 0$$

The value of φ will be passed to the output layer as predicted value y'.

Step 4. Now we calculate mean squared error using Eq. 3 by replacing the values of y' = 0 (predicted value) and y = 0 (ground truth) as mentioned in table 1.

$$C = \frac{1}{2}(0 - 0)^2$$

$$C = 0$$

As the value of C is minimum therefore, we will save these weights and repeat Step 2 – 4 for another input of table 1 that is x1 = 0 and x2 = 1 (Fig. 2.6).

Bias Value

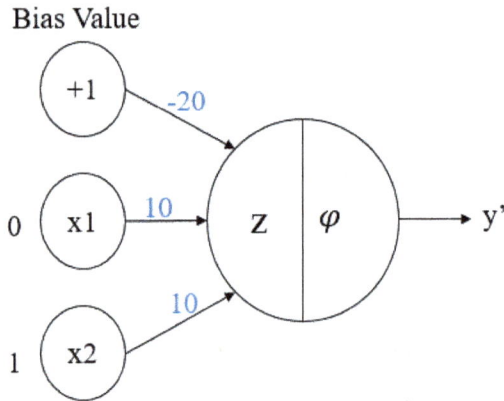

Fig. 2.6 Neural network to predict output for input x1 = 0 and x2 = 1.

Step 2. Calculate z using Eq. 1.

$$z = 1 * (-20) + 0 * 10 + 1 * 10$$

$$z = -10$$

Step 3. Calculate the value of z using threshold activation function. Therefore,

$$\varphi = f(-10)$$

$$\varphi = 0$$

The value of φ will be passed to the output layer as predicted value y'.

Step 4. Now we calculate mean squared error using Eq. 3 by replacing the values of y' = 0 (predicted value) and y = 0 (ground truth) as mention in the table 1.

$$C = \frac{1}{2}(0-0)^2$$

$$C = 0$$

As the value of C is minimum therefore, we will save these weights and repeat Step 2 – 4 for another input of table 1 that is x1 = 1 and x2 = 0 (Fig. 2.7).

Bias Value

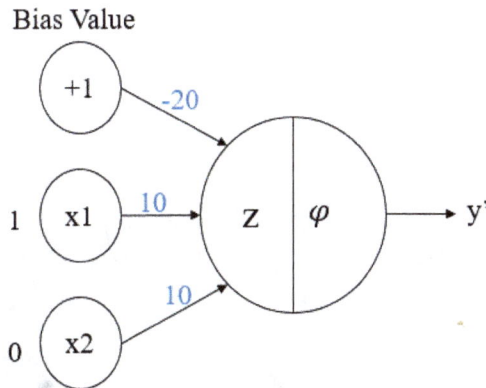

Fig. 2.7. Neural network to predict output for input x1 = 1 and x2 = 0.

Step 2. Calculate z using Eq. 1.

$$z = 1 * (-20) + 1 * 10 + 0 * 10$$

$$z = -10$$

Step 3. Calculate the value of z using threshold activation function. Therefore,

$$\varphi = f(-10)$$

$$\varphi = 0$$

The value of φ will be passed to the output layer as predicted value y'.

Step 4. Now we calculate mean squared error using Eq. 3 by replacing the values of y' = 0 (predicted value) and y = 0 (ground truth) as mention in the table 1.

$$C = \frac{1}{2}(0 - 0)^2$$

$$C = 0$$

As the value of C is minimum therefore, we will save these weights and repeat Step 2 – 4 for another input of table 1 that is x1 = 1 and x2 = 1 (Fig. 2.8).

Bias Value

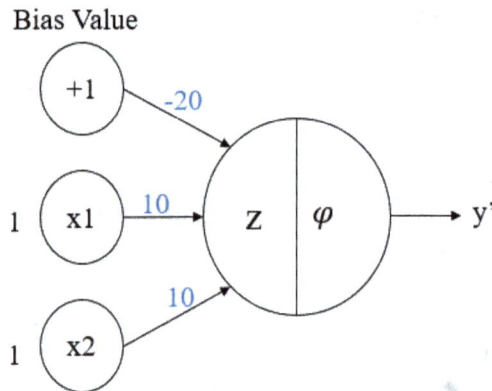

Fig. 2.8 Neural network to predict output for input x1 = 1 and x2 = 1.

Step 2. Calculate z using Eq. 1.

$$z = 1 * (-20) + 1 * 10 + 1 * 10$$

$$z = 0$$

Step 3. Calculate the value of z using threshold activation function. Therefore,

$$\varphi = f(0)$$

$$\varphi = 1$$

The value of φ will be passed to the output layer as predicted value y'.

Step 4. Now we calculate mean squared error using Eq. 3 by replacing the values of y' = 1 (predicted value) and y = 1 (ground truth) as mention in the table 1.

$$C = \frac{1}{2}(1 - 1)^2$$

$$C = 0$$

As the value of C is minimum therefore, we can say that our model with weights w_b = **- 20**,
w_1 = **+10**, and w_2 = **+10** working accurately for AND logic gate.

Summary

Artificial Neural Network (ANN) is multi-layered computational model that comprises of computational unit called neuron. ANN based model have two compulsory layers that are input and output layer. Moreover, can have multiple hidden layers according to the application.

Each layer of ANN receive input from the previous layer (except input layer) and pass the output to another connected layer. ANN model is train using training data that is the major portion of complete dataset (generally 80% of dataset) using backpropagation technique. Some of the major applications of ANN are image or text classification, object recognition, and speech recognition.

Exercises

1. What do you understand by dependent and independent variables in a dataset?
2. Explain how the artificial neural network related to actual brain structure.
3. What is perceptron?

4. Consider an ANN based model with input/output layer and one hidden layer. Explain the procedure of backpropagation, assuming the initial assign weights as all +1.
5. What are the major areas of application of ANN?
6. Explain the use of loss function in the process of back propagation?
7. Explain the role of activation function in ANN.

3

Implementation of Artificial Neural Network in python

In this chapter, we will implement the ANN using a dataset Churn_Modelling.csv available on Kaggle.com. The dataset store the information about the bank customer including the ex-customers. The dependent variable that is the last column ('Exited') of the dataset containing the binary values. Dictating whether the customer is still associated with the bank or not. We will build an ANN model using this dataset to predict whether the customer will close the account or not. The dataset is having 10,000 rows and 14 columns in which we will use some appropriate columns (features) for training purpose.

Firstly, we import the important libraries

```
import numpy as np
import pandas as pd
import tensorflow as tf
```

Now, we read the Churn_Modelling.csv file into a dataframe using pandas. Further will check whether the dataframe is having any null values or not as mention in the second line of below code. Also print the total null values in each column using dataset.isnull().sum() function. With the last line dataset.shape the number of rows and columns will be displayed. In this case we are not having any null values in the dataset and the shape of the dataset is (10000, 14).

```
dataset = pd.read_csv('Churn_Modelling.csv')
print(dataset.isnull().values.any())
print(dataset.isnull().sum())
print(dataset.shape)
```

Now we extract X, y from the dataset for training and testing purpose. For X we have selected all rows for all the columns (features) from index 3 that is 'CreditScore'. For y the last column labeled 'Exited' is

selected containing the corresponding ground truth values. The iloc()
function enables us to retrieve the rows from the dataframe using the
index instead of column name.

```
X = dataset.iloc[:, 3:-1].values
y = dataset.iloc[:, -1].values
```

As the dataset is having some categorical data which is to be transformed into numeric values before using it to train the ANN model.
Therefore, LabelEncoder used for encoding 'Gender' column and converting the male/female labels into binary. In the below code, LabelEncoder class is imported from the sklearn library and le object is
created for the class. Further, fit_transform function used to apply the
encoding over all the rows of column index 2 ('Gender').

```
from sklearn.preprocessing import LabelEncoder
le = LabelEncoder()
X[:, 2] = le.fit_transform(X[:, 2])
```

Still the data X is having categorical data representing the 'Geography'
in the dataset. To transform this data we have used OneHoTEncoder
technique with ColumnTransformer instead of LabelEncoder. Using
ColumnTransformer class it is not required to use LableEncoder before OneHotEncoder. For this purpose, both the classes that is OneHotEncoder and ColumnTransformer imported from sk.learn library.
While creating the object of the ColumnTransformer class we pass
some parameters. These parameters representing that OneHotEncoder is to be applied on column indexed 1 in X and rest of the column
will remain same (remainder="passthrough"). So, when we use
fit_transform function with the object of ColumnTransformer that is
ct then only the values of column 1 will get transformed. Rest all the
column values remain intact and converted to numpy array as shown
in the last line of the code below.

```python
from sklearn.preprocessing import OneHotEncoder
from sklearn.compose import ColumnTransformer
ct = ColumnTransformer([("encoder",
                         OneHotEncoder(),[1])],
                        remainder="passthrough")
X = np.array(ct.fit_transform(X))
```

As we have done with the required pre-processing of the data so we can split the data for training and testing purpose as shown in below code. Class train_test_split from library sklearn used for splitting the data. During split process 80% of the data is reserved to train the ANN model and rest 20% for testing the accuracy of the model (test_size = 0.2). As mention in the below code, (X_train, y_train) will be used for training of ANN model and (X_test, y_test) for testing the accuracy of the trained model. By taking random_state = 0, the training and testing sets remain same for different executions.

```python
from sklearn.model_selection import train_test_split
X_train, X_test, y_train, y_test = train_test_split(X, y,
                                          test_size = 0.2,
                                          random_state = 0)
```

Now we standardize the training data within a certain range using StandardScaler class from sklearn library to optimize the computation.

```python
from sklearn.preprocessing import StandardScaler
sc = StandardScaler()
X_train = sc.fit_transform(X_train)
X_test = sc.transform(X_test)
```

After standardizing the data, we build neural network model using tensorflow with keras API (Application Programming Interface). Sequential class is used to group the layers of neural network into a model (ann in this case).

```python
ann = tf.keras.models.Sequential()
```

Using add() function we can add the layers in the model. As shown in below code two hidden layers are added into the model named ann. Each intermediate layers (hidden layers) are having 6 neurons and ReLU used as an activation function. We can add any number of intermediate layers in the model according to our requirement. Input layer is not required to be explicitly mention in the model. The dense() function is used to create fully connected hidden layers that is each node of layer one is connected to every node of another layer.

```
ann.add(tf.keras.layers.Dense(units=6, activation='relu'))
ann.add(tf.keras.layers.Dense(units=6, activation='relu'))
```

Further, an output layer added into the model. Output layer is having single unit and sigmoid activation function for predicting binary result.

```
ann.add(tf.keras.layers.Dense(units=1, activation='sigmoid'))
```

After creating the model, compile() function is used for model configuration before training the model. In addition, to define optimizer, loss function and metrics for predicting result. In our model, we have used 'adam' optimizer for iteratively updating weights of network according to the training data. Binary_crossentropy is used for computing loss between the ground truth and the predicted result. Binary_crossentropy loss function used in the model that give binary results. Further, accuracy is used as metric to judge the performance of the model as shown in the below code.

```
ann.compile(optimizer = 'adam',
            loss = 'binary_crossentropy',
            metrics = ['accuracy'])
```

Now we train the model (ann) using training data (X_train, y_train) with batch size of 32 and 100 epochs. Where, batch size means the number of samples processed through the model at once during training process. Moreover, when the entire training data passed through the network and weights are adjusted accordingly is known as one epoch. The fit() function is used to train the model for 100 epochs in this case.

```
ann.fit(X_train, y_train, batch_size = 32, epochs = 100)
```

After training the model, predict function used for predicting the performance of the model over test data (X_test). As the predicted values will be continuous value, therefore the values are converted into binary by considering 1 for all values greater than 0.5. However, rest of the values will be considered as 0.

```
y_pred = ann.predict(X_test)
y_pred = (y_pred > 0.5)
print(y_pred)
```

To understand the performance of the model we can calculate the confusion matrix and accuracy score by importing confusion_matrix, accuracy_score class from sklearn library as shown in below code. Confusion matrix is basically a summary of correctly and incorrectly predicted results by the model in the tabular format. It computes true positive (TP), true negative (TN), false positive (FP) and false negative (FN). TP and TN are the number of predicted values matching with corresponding value under dependent variable y (ground truth). FP and FN are the total number of not matching predicted results. Accuracy score gives the mean accuracy of the model for test data which is 85.65% in this case.

True positive are correctly predicted positive values by the model, according to the test samples (y_test in this case).

True Negative are correctly predicted negative values by the model, according to the test samples.

False positive are incorrectly predicted positive values by the model, according to the test samples.

False Negative are incorrectly predicted negative values by the model, according to the test samples.

```
from sklearn.metrics import confusion_matrix, accuracy_score
cm = confusion_matrix(y_test, y_pred)
print(cm)
accuracy_score(y_test, y_pred)
```

Now we will see all the above lines of code together in below Example 1 with corresponding outputs. In Example 1, all the above snippets mentioned as a single program and output of all snippets are also shown for better understanding.

```
[ ]  import numpy as np
     import pandas as pd
     import tensorflow as tf
```

```
[ ]  dataset = pd.read_csv('Churn_Modelling.csv')
     print(dataset.isnull().values.any())
     print(dataset.isnull().sum())
     print(dataset.shape)
```

```
False
RowNumber          0
CustomerId         0
Surname            0
CreditScore        0
Geography          0
Gender             0
Age                0
Tenure             0
Balance            0
NumOfProducts      0
HasCrCard          0
IsActiveMember     0
EstimatedSalary    0
Exited             0
dtype: int64
(10000, 14)
```

```
[ ]  #Lets seperate X and y from the dataset
     X = dataset.iloc[:, 3:-1].values
     y = dataset.iloc[:, -1].values
```

```
[ ]  print(X)

     [[619 'France' 'Female' ... 1 1 101348.88]
      [608 'Spain' 'Female' ... 0 1 112542.58]
      [502 'France' 'Female' ... 1 0 113931.57]
      ...
      [709 'France' 'Female' ... 0 1 42085.58]
      [772 'Germany' 'Male' ... 1 0 92888.52]
      [792 'France' 'Female' ... 1 0 38190.78]]
```

```
[ ]  #Lable encoder for Gender
     from sklearn.preprocessing import LabelEncoder
     le = LabelEncoder()
     X[:, 2] = le.fit_transform(X[:, 2])
```

```
[ ]  print(X)

     [[619 'France' 0 ... 1 1 101348.88]
      [608 'Spain' 0 ... 0 1 112542.58]
      [502 'France' 0 ... 1 0 113931.57]
      ...
      [709 'France' 0 ... 0 1 42085.58]
      [772 'Germany' 1 ... 1 0 92888.52]
      [792 'France' 0 ... 1 0 38190.78]]
```

```
[ ]  #One Hot Encoding the "Geography" column
     from sklearn.compose import ColumnTransformer
     from sklearn.preprocessing import OneHotEncoder
     ct = ColumnTransformer(transformers=[('encoder',
                                  OneHotEncoder(), [1])],
                                  remainder='passthrough')
     X = np.array(ct.fit_transform(X))
```

```
[ ]  print(X)

     [[1.0 0.0 0.0 ... 1 1 101348.88]
      [0.0 0.0 1.0 ... 0 1 112542.58]
      [1.0 0.0 0.0 ... 1 0 113931.57]
      ...
      [1.0 0.0 0.0 ... 0 1 42085.58]
      [0.0 1.0 0.0 ... 1 0 92888.52]
      [1.0 0.0 0.0 ... 1 0 38190.78]]
```

```
[ ]  #Splitting the dataset into the Training set and Test set
     from sklearn.model_selection import train_test_split
     X_train, X_test, y_train, y_test = train_test_split(X, y,
                                  test_size = 0.2,
                                  random_state = 0)
```

```
[ ]  #Feature Scaling
     from sklearn.preprocessing import StandardScaler
     sc = StandardScaler()
     X_train = sc.fit_transform(X_train)
     X_test = sc.transform(X_test)
```

```
[ ]  print(X_train)

     [[-1.01460667 -0.5698444   1.74309049 ...  0.64259497 -1.03227043
        1.10643166]
      [-1.01460667  1.75486502 -0.57369368 ...  0.64259497  0.9687384
       -0.74866447]
      [ 0.98560362 -0.5698444  -0.57369368 ...  0.64259497 -1.03227043
        1.48533467]
      ...
      [ 0.98560362 -0.5698444  -0.57369368 ...  0.64259497 -1.03227043
        1.41231994]
      [-1.01460667 -0.5698444   1.74309049 ...  0.64259497  0.9687384
        0.84432121]
      [-1.01460667  1.75486502 -0.57369368 ...  0.64259497 -1.03227043
        0.32472465]]
```

```
[ ]  #Initializing Artificial Neural Network Model
     ann = tf.keras.models.Sequential()
     #Two hidden layers
     ann.add(tf.keras.layers.Dense(units=6, activation='relu'))
     ann.add(tf.keras.layers.Dense(units=6, activation='relu'))
     #output layer
     ann.add(tf.keras.layers.Dense(units=1, activation='sigmoid'))


[ ]  #Compiling the ANN
     ann.compile(optimizer = 'adam',
                 loss = 'binary_crossentropy',
                 metrics = ['accuracy'])
```

```
[ ]  #Training the ANN model on the Training set
     ann.fit(X_train, y_train, batch_size = 32, epochs = 100)

     Epoch 1/100
     250/250 [==============================] - 1s 2ms/step - loss: 0.5399 - accuracy: 0.7889
     Epoch 2/100
     250/250 [==============================] - 0s 2ms/step - loss: 0.4663 - accuracy: 0.7989
     Epoch 3/100
     250/250 [==============================] - 0s 2ms/step - loss: 0.4405 - accuracy: 0.8086
     Epoch 4/100
     250/250 [==============================] - 0s 2ms/step - loss: 0.4285 - accuracy: 0.8176
     Epoch 5/100
     250/250 [==============================] - 0s 2ms/step - loss: 0.4229 - accuracy: 0.8219
     Epoch 6/100
     250/250 [==============================] - 0s 2ms/step - loss: 0.4190 - accuracy: 0.8248
     Epoch 7/100
     250/250 [==============================] - 0s 2ms/step - loss: 0.4159 - accuracy: 0.8267
     Epoch 8/100
     250/250 [==============================] - 0s 2ms/step - loss: 0.4143 - accuracy: 0.8266
     Epoch 9/100
     250/250 [==============================] - 0s 2ms/step - loss: 0.4118 - accuracy: 0.8270
     Epoch 10/100
     250/250 [==============================] - 0s 2ms/step - loss: 0.4094 - accuracy: 0.8275
     Epoch 11/100
     250/250 [==============================] - 0s 2ms/step - loss: 0.4070 - accuracy: 0.8282
     Epoch 12/100
     250/250 [==============================] - 0s 2ms/step - loss: 0.4040 - accuracy: 0.8285
     Epoch 13/100
     250/250 [==============================] - 0s 2ms/step - loss: 0.4009 - accuracy: 0.8276
```

```
[ ]  #Predicting the Test set results
     y_pred = ann.predict(X_test)
     y_pred = (y_pred > 0.5)
     print(y_pred)

     [[False]
      [False]
      [False]
      ...
      [False]
      [False]
      [False]]
```

```
#Confusion Matrix and accuracy score
from sklearn.metrics import confusion_matrix, accuracy_score
cm = confusion_matrix(y_test, y_pred)
print(cm)
accuracy_score(y_test, y_pred)
```

```
[[1487  108]
 [ 179  226]]
0.8565
```

4

Introduction to Convolutional Neural Network

Convolutional Neural Network (CNN) is the concept of deep learning, which mainly use in image classification. For example, classification of diseased crops, hand-written number/alphabet classification, classification of roads or other objects in satellite images, etc. Also used in object detection and analysis of medical images.

CNN, can be considered as the advanced version of ANN with automating the process of feature extraction. The main steps of CNN model are process of convolution with multiple kernels, activation function, pooling, flattening, and fully connected dense network. In this chapter, we will discuss the introduction to all the operations involved in CNN. However, in upcoming chapters the convolution and pooling operation of CNN discussed in detail. The complete diagram of CNN model shown in Fig. 4.1. In which, image is given as input for convolution process that is followed by activation and pooling operation. Further, the resultant matrix is flatten into a vector that is given as input to fully connected dense network. In the output layer of dense network, softmax activation function used for multiple classification or sigmoid use for binary classification. By the term, multiple classification we mean that the dataset is having images of more than two categories to be classified for example classification of numbers from 0 to 9. However, binary classification we mean that dataset is having only two type of images to be classified for example classification of dog and cat.

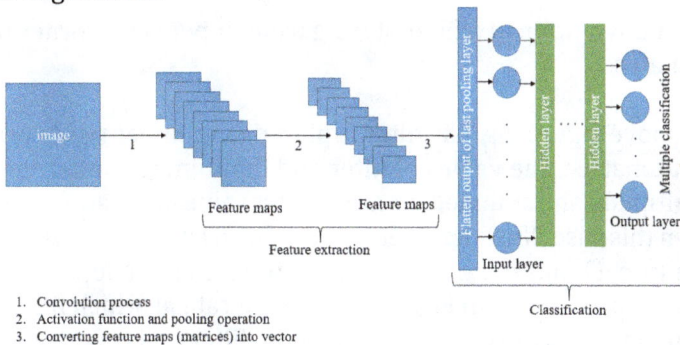

1. Convolution process
2. Activation function and pooling operation
3. Converting feature maps (matrices) into vector

Fig. 4.1 CNN Model

4.1 Convolution Process

Convolution is the process of convolving multiple filters (matrices) over input images to extract important features (information) from the images. These features further used to train the model for accurate classification of unknown images with similar features. Various filters are convolve over images to extract more and more prominent features to train the model. This process of convolution over an input matrix gives a matrix with some important information called feature maps (with reduced dimensions). Feature maps are the matrices with some useful information about the input images (matrix) such as edges, color, shape, texture, etc.

In the convolution process pixel values of the input image under a filter are multiplied and summed up to a single value. Further, the filter convolved over the full input image to cover all pixels. For better understanding of convolution process, let's take an example to convolve small filter over a matrix.

Considering an input image of size n = 5x5 and kernel (filter) of size f = 3x3. Therefore, resultant feature map will be of size (n-f+1) x (n-f+1) that is 3x3.

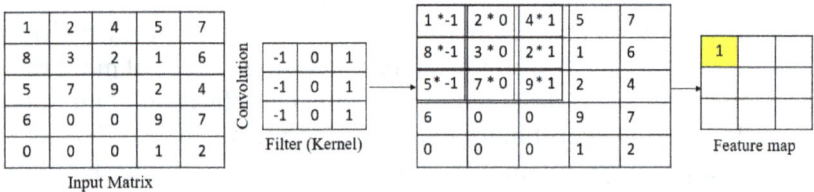

Fig. 4.2 Convolution of a filter staring from upper right corner of an input matrix.

In the above, figure Fig. 4.2, filter is placed over upper right corner of an input matrix. The values of filter and input image under the filter are multiplied and summed up to give first value of a feature map that is one in this case. Now the filter is slide ahead skipping single column (stride rate 1) and the process repeat to calculate another value of feature map as shown in Fig. 4.3. Stride is a rate at which filter move over an input image. If stride = 2, then the filter will traverse over an input matrix by skipping 2 columns instead of one.

1	2	4	5	7
8	3	2	1	6
5	7	9	2	4
6	0	0	9	7
0	0	0	1	2

Input Matrix

Convolution

-1	0	1
-1	0	1
-1	0	1

Filter (Kernel)

1	2 *-1	4 * 0	5 * 1	7
8	3 *-1	2 * 0	1 * 1	6
5	7 * -1	9 * 0	2 * 1	4
6	0	0	9	7
0	0	0	1	2

1	-4	

Feature map

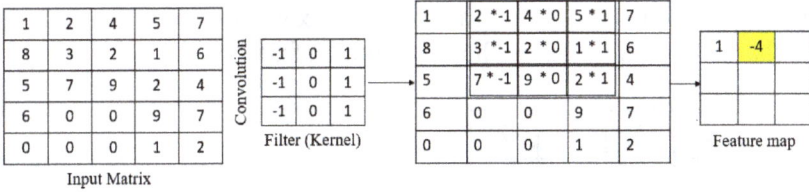

Fig. 4.3 Convolution of filter over next portion of an input image by skipping one column.

Similarly, filter move ahead and calculate third value of the feature map as shown in Fig. 4.4.

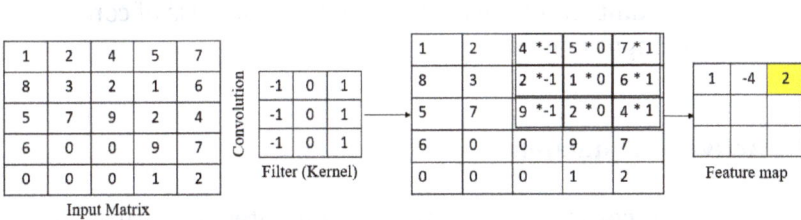

1	2	4	5	7
8	3	2	1	6
5	7	9	2	4
6	0	0	9	7
0	0	0	1	2

Input Matrix

Convolution

-1	0	1
-1	0	1
-1	0	1

Filter (Kernel)

1	2	4 *-1	5 * 0	7 * 1
8	3	2 *-1	1 * 0	6 * 1
5	7	9 *-1	2 * 0	4 * 1
6	0	0	9	7
0	0	0	1	2

1	-4	2

Feature map

Fig. 4.4 Convolution process of 3x3 filter over 5x5 input matrix.

After completing the convolution process for last column, now the filter will move down by one row to convolve further. As shown in the Fig. 4.5. filter is placed in the beginning of second row to traverse ahead for calculating other values of filter matrix.

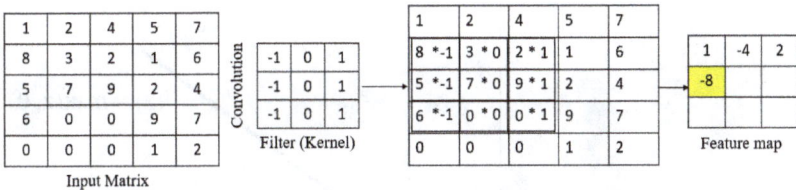

1	2	4	5	7
8	3	2	1	6
5	7	9	2	4
6	0	0	9	7
0	0	0	1	2

Input Matrix

Convolution

-1	0	1
-1	0	1
-1	0	1

Filter (Kernel)

1	2	4	5	7
8 *-1	3 * 0	2 * 1	1	6
5 *-1	7 * 0	9 * 1	2	4
6 *-1	0 * 0	0 * 1	9	7
0	0	0	1	2

1	-4	2
-8		

Feature map

Fig. 4.5 Convolution process starting from the beginning of an input matrix skipping the first row.

Now the similar process of convolution will continue and give resultant feature map as shown in Fig. 4.6. In convolution process, the number of filters are always equal to the number of channels in the input image. If the shape of input image is n x n x y, where y is the number of channels than the filter shape should be f x f x y.

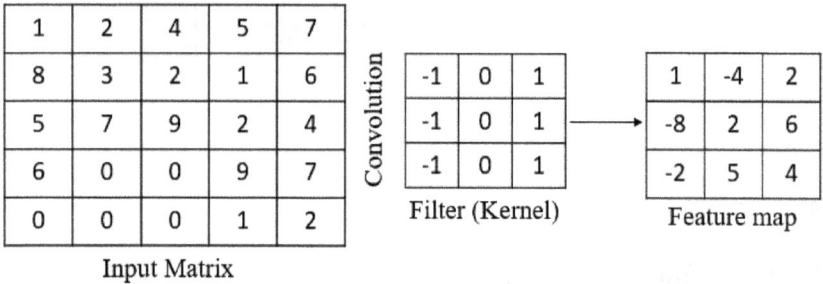

1	2	4	5	7
8	3	2	1	6
5	7	9	2	4
6	0	0	9	7
0	0	0	1	2

Input Matrix

Convolution

-1	0	1
-1	0	1
-1	0	1

Filter (Kernel)

1	-4	2
-8	2	6
-2	5	4

Feature map

Fig. 4.6. Resultant feature map after complete process of convolution over an input matrix.

4.2 Activation Function

In CNN after convolution operation, generated feature maps are passed to rectified linear unit (ReLU) activation function. ReLU is simple to compute. It just pass all positive values of feature map as it is and replace negative values to 0 as shown in Fig. 4.7. Application to ReLU enhance the non-linearity in the feature maps to train the model for more complex features. Further, it reduce the possibility of vanishing gradient descent.

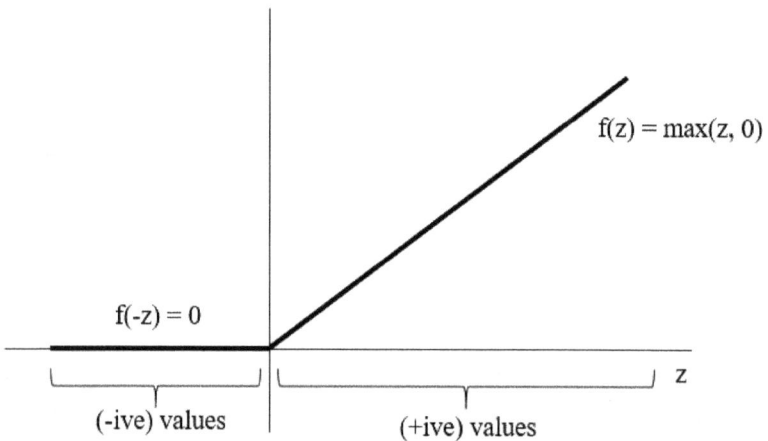

$f(z) = \max(z, 0)$

$f(-z) = 0$

(-ive) values

(+ive) values

z

Fig. 4.7 ReLU activation function.

With multiple advantages of ReLU over other activation function such as tanh and sigmoid, ReLU has become a default activation function in any convolutional network. It provide both linearity and non-linearity to the model. ReLU is linear for all positive values whereas non-linear for all negative values. Linearity required for fast computation and non-linearity required for robust training of the model. Further, ReLU activation function provide absolute zero values which make model computationally fast and ease the optimization process.

4.3 Pooling

In CNN we generally use max pooling operation. Pooling used to down sample the features maps generated after the convolution process. In simple words down sampling is reducing the size of input matrix. The major disadvantage of feature maps is the position sensitive features. That means the extracted features from the input images using convolution operation are basically contain the information about the position of particular feature in the input image. Such as feature map of dog image also contain the information about the position of eye of the dog in actual image. Therefore, if we use only feature maps to train the model then for any flipped or rotated input image model may perform inadequately. Pooling make the feature maps independent from the positional information about the features of the input image and at the same time retaining other important information required to train the model. Pooling layer is used after the convolutional layers and activation function. Pooling is performed over each feature map and generate same number of the down sampled feature maps. For example, after the convolution process if we are having 100 feature maps than the entire feature maps are pooled and we get 100 down sample feature maps. In pooling operation, mostly a filter of size 2x2 is convolved over a feature map with stride rate of 2. That means if the feature map is of size 12x12 (144 pixel values) than after pooling with 2x2 filter and stride of 2 the down sampled feature map would be of size 6x6 (36 pixel values). Down-sampling of the feature maps makes the model computationally optimized.

In max pooling, a patch or filter is convolved over a feature map. Further, with each traverse the maximum value of the feature maps under the patch is taken as pooled feature. The process of max pooling shown from Fig. 4.8 to Fig 4.11. In Fig. 4.8. patch of 2x2 is convolve over the first quadrant of the feature map and maximum value that is

8 in this case is pooled from the feature map. Now 8 become the first value of the resultant pooled feature map with reduced size. Similarly, the patch is traverse ahead with stride = 2 as shown in Fig. 4.9. Stride = 2 means, the patch will move ahead by skipping the two columns of the feature map. In the same way, the feature map is down sampled to the size of 2x2 containing the salient features of the input image.

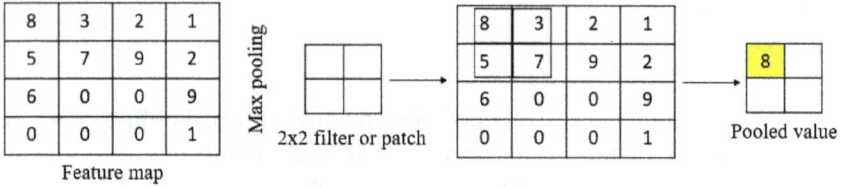

8	3	2	1
5	7	9	2
6	0	0	9
0	0	0	1

Feature map

Max pooling

2x2 filter or patch

8	3	2	1
5	7	9	2
6	0	0	9
0	0	0	1

8	

Pooled value

Fig. 4.8 Pooling the maximum value from the values under the patch of 2x2.

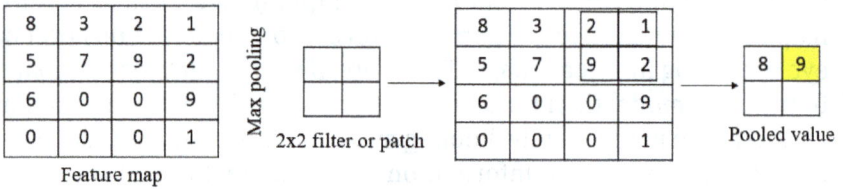

8	3	2	1
5	7	9	2
6	0	0	9
0	0	0	1

Feature map

Max pooling

2x2 filter or patch

8	3	2	1
5	7	9	2
6	0	0	9
0	0	0	1

8	9

Pooled value

Fig. 4.9 Extracting another maximum value among the values of the feature map under the patch.

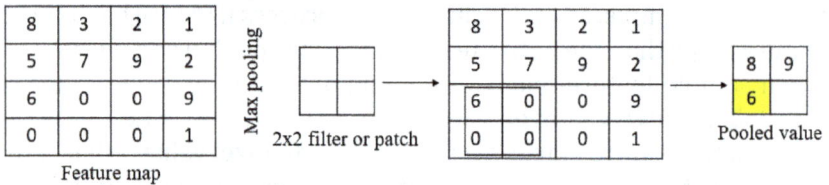

8	3	2	1
5	7	9	2
6	0	0	9
0	0	0	1

Feature map

Max pooling

2x2 filter or patch

8	3	2	1
5	7	9	2
6	0	0	9
0	0	0	1

8	9
6	

Pooled value

Fig. 4.10 Extracting third value of pooled feature map.

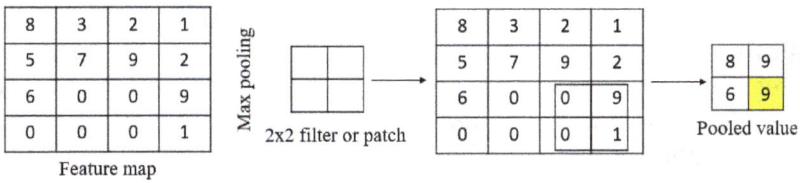

Fig. 4.11. Final down sampled pooled feature map.

4.4 Flattening and Fully Connected Artificial Neural Network

After extracting and down sampling all the feature maps, now it's time for classification. All the pooled feature maps are flatten into a vector (nx1). Flattening of a matrix is the process of rearranging all rows of matrix vertically one after another as shown in Fig. 4.12. The matrix of size of 3x3 is converted into a vector of size length 9.

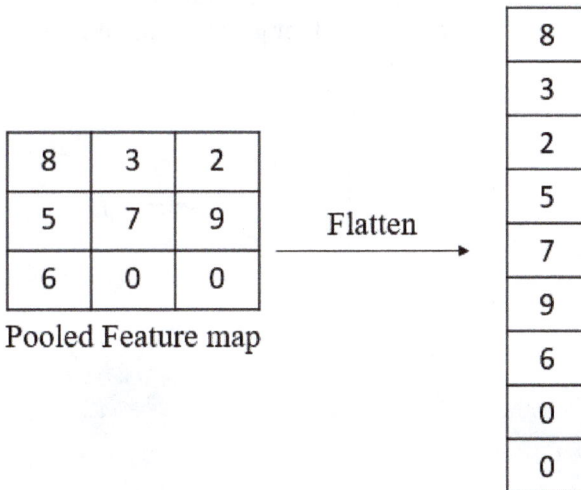

Fig. 4.12 Flattening of pooled feature map.

The flatten feature maps are given as input to the fully connected artificial neural network to train the model for classification. The number of neurons in the input layer of the fully connected neural network are always remain equal to the length of feature vector. Whereas the number of neurons in the output layer are equal to the number of classes to be classified. That is the number of categories in the training dataset for example dataset of dog and cat is having to categories of images. Further, a numeric MNIST dataset is having 10 categories or classes of image that is from 0 to 9. The output layer of the fully connected neural network use sigmoid and softmax activation function for binary and multiple (multi-class) classification respectively.

Sigmoid activation function is also known as logistic activation function. The mathematical formula of the activation function in shown below in Eq. 1.

$$f(z) = \frac{1}{1 + e^{-z}} \qquad (1)$$

Where z is the input to sigmoid function and e is the Euler's number. Further, the graph of the activation function is shown in Fig. 4.13. According to the graph, the resultant value of the sigmoid activation function always remain in the range from 0 to 1. For higher negative values it remain close to zero and for greater positive values it remain close to 1.

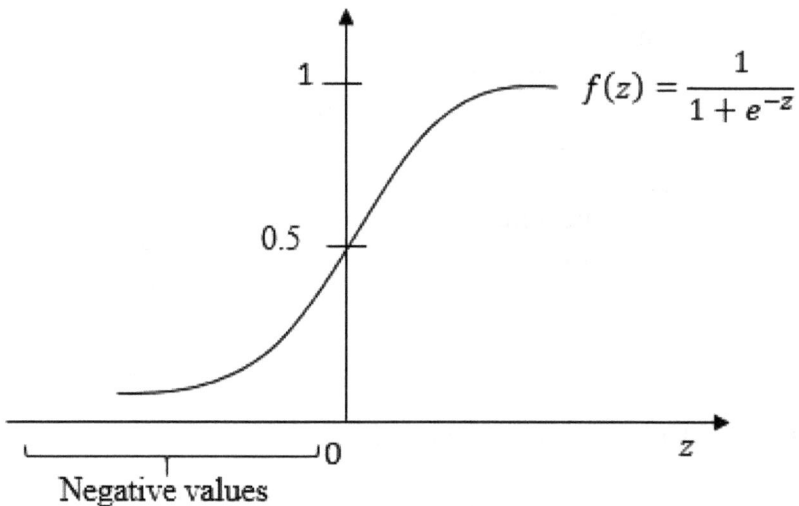

Fig. 4.13 Graph representing sigmoid activation function.

Sigmoid activation function use in output layer of fully connected neural network for the purpose of binary classification. Function convert the real number into the corresponding probability to depict the strength of hypothesis (predicted value) for particular input. For example, in dog/cat classification dataset the neural network would have two neurons in the output layer representing dog and cat class respectively. In this case, the sigmoid activation function in the output layer of the network will return corresponding probability for received real number. The neuron with higher probability can be considered as the predicted output for input features as shown in Fig. 4.14. In which a dog image is given to network for classification and network classify the input image correctly as the sigmoid activation function in the output layer return higher value to the neuron representing the dog class. Therefore, the predicted result by the network can be considered as correct for the particular input.

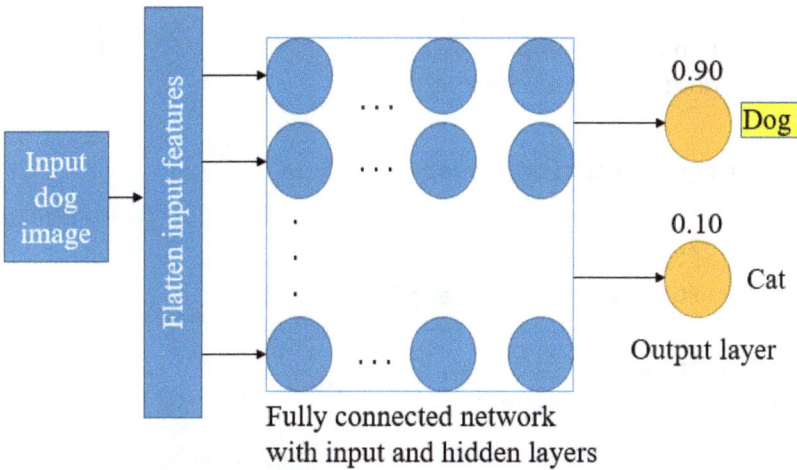

Fig. 4.14 Result of trained network for input dog image.

Softmax activation function used for the classification purpose when the number of classes in the training dataset is more than two. That means the network basically return the vector of real numbers instead of single value. Softmax activation function convert the vector of real number into the probability vector representing the strength of predicted outputs for each class. The mathematical formula for activation function shown in Eq. 2.

$$f(z_i) = \frac{e^{z_i}}{\sum_{j=1}^{k} e^{z_j}} \qquad (2)$$

Where z represent the vector of real numbers.

Example 1 show the python code of softmax activation function. Converting list of real numbers into vector of probabilities with user defined softmax function. Which is accepting a list of real numbers as parameter and returning the list containing the corresponding probability of each number. The returned probability list stored in variable 'result'. In last two lines 'result' is displayed showing the list of corresponding probabilities and sum of all elements of 'result' is also displayed which is equal to 1. The scientific notations suppressed while displaying the results with the following line.
np.set_printoptions(suppress=True)

```python
import numpy as np
from numpy import exp

np.set_printoptions(suppress=True)

def softmax(vec):
    return exp(vec) / exp(vec).sum()

vec = np.array([10, 20, 15])
result = softmax(vec)

print(result)
print(result.sum())

[0.00004509 0.99326236 0.00669255]
1.0
```

Example 1. Implementation of softmax activation function.

Summary

CNN has automate the process of feature extraction, which is done manually in case of artificial neural network based models. CNN majorly used for image classification. It involve process of convolution followed by activation function and pooling operation, to extract the features from input images. These features are given as input to fully connected network for final classification. In convolution process, multiple small size filters (kernels) convolved over input images. Further, dot product of kernels values and the pixel values of input image under kernel is calculate with each shift of kernel matrix. In this way, important features are extracted from input images. The resultant matrix of convolution process in called feature map.

These feature maps further passed to the ReLU activation function, which is simple to compute and fast. It enhance non-linearity in the feature maps, which help in robust training of the model. Feature maps generated by the convolution process are position dependent. It means that features extracted from the input image depends on the position of that feature in input image. To overcome this drawback, max-pooling process is used. In max-pooling a small window (generally 2x2) convolve over feature map to extract the maximum value among the values under the window. Further, the pooling process down-sample the feature maps to enhance the computation and extract more dense features. These features are given as input to fully connected artificial neural network for final classification.

Questions

1. Explain the process of CNN.
2. What are the major advantages of CNN?
3. Explain the convolution process using a kernel 'k' of size 3x3 on a matrix 'm' of size 5x5 as shown below.
   k = [[-1, 0, 1],   m = [[1, 2, 3, 4, 5],
        [-1, 0, 1],   [6, 7, 8, 9, 0],
        [-1, 0, 1]]   [2, 3, 4, 5, 1],
                             [4, 5, 4, 5, 4],
                             [2, 2, 1, 1, 3]]

4. How ReLU activation function provide both linearity and non-linearity to the feature maps. Explain with the help of example.

5. Perform the max-pooling and average pooling on the matrix 'm' as mentioned in question 3, and consider 2x2 window for pooling.

5

Convolution Process

Convolution word include the word convolve and dictionary meaning of convolve is to roll over. Therefore, the key idea behind the process of convolution is to convolve multiple kernels over an image to have multiple images with difference features of input image. Grey scale image or image with single channel can be considered as 2D matrix also. Whereas, color images (RGB images) represent the volume of three matrices stack together. In this chapter, we will see the process of convolution with 2D matrix or a grey scale image. Further, we also discuss the convolution operation over volume or color image (RGB). The main objective of convolution process is to automate the process of feature extraction. The extracted features used to train the model for predicting results for unknown inputs.

5.1 Feature Extraction

Features of an image are information about an image or description about an image. Considering an image of a dog, than the color, shape, nose, eyes, legs, etc are all describing about the features of the dog. Features of various images in the dataset, used to train a model for the purpose classification. One of the simple method is to consider each pixel value as feature of an image. Considering a gray-scale image and converting it into array as shown in Example 1. In which, the size of an image is (1152, 864) that is total number of pixels would be 1152 * 864 = 995328. Therefore, the number of features will also be equal to 995328. However, we cannot trained a model with a single image, therefore assuming that a dataset is having 1000 images. Then in that case, total number of features would be 995328000. In more simple terms, if we convert dataset into csv file than there will be 1000 rows representing number of images and 995328 number of columns representing features of images in dataset. Therefore, one of the obvious drawback of considering raw pixel values as features of an image is large and unmanageable number of features. Therefore, one better way is to consider only important and useful information of an image such as edges, color, texture, etc. To extract these features from each image we can use multiple kernels, kernel is nothing but a small matrix with certain values. The python codes for extracting some features from an image using kernels are shown in below examples.

```
import cv2
from skimage.io import imshow
```

```
img1 = cv2.imread("meandkunkun.jpeg", 0)
```

```
print(img1.shape)
```

```
(1152, 864)
```

```
print(img1)
```

```
[[ 34  34  34 ...  52  51  51]
 [ 33  33  33 ...  52  51  51]
 [ 31  31  31 ...  52  51  51]
 ...
 [135 136 137 ... 171 170 170]
 [134 135 137 ... 163 162 162]
 [133 134 137 ... 156 156 155]]
```

```
flat_img1 = img1.flatten()
print(flat_img1.shape)
```

```
(995328,)
```

Example 1. Calculating number of raw pixel values in an image.

In Example 2 vertical edges are extracted from an image using a kernel matrix as shown below.

$$M1 \quad = \quad \begin{matrix} [[1, 0, -1], \\ [1, 0, -1], \\ [1, 0, -1]] \end{matrix}$$

Similarly, in Example 3 horizontal edges are extracted from an image using 3x3 matrix (kernel) as shown below.

$$M2 \quad = \quad \begin{matrix} [[1, 1, 1], \\ [0, 0, 0], \\ [-1, -1, -1]] \end{matrix}$$

```python
import cv2
import numpy as np
from skimage.io import imshow
```

```python
image = cv2.imread("meandkunkun.jpeg",0)
image = cv2.resize(image,(64, 64))
imshow(image)
```

```
<matplotlib.image.AxesImage at 0x257ac11b280>
```

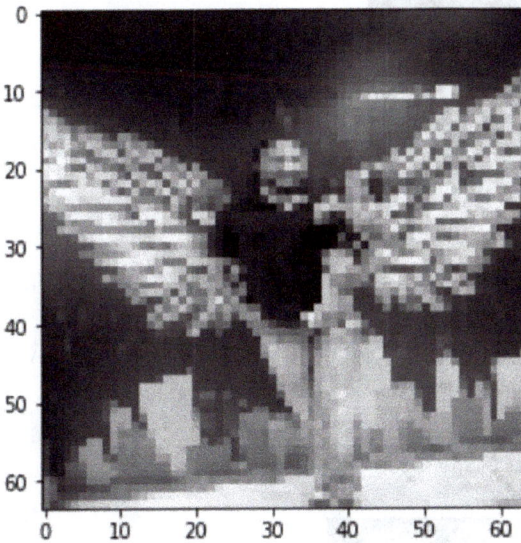

```
vertical = np.array([[1, 0, -1], [1, 0, -1], [1, 0, -1]])
image_hor = cv2.filter2D(image,-1,vertical)
imshow(image_hor)
```

```
<matplotlib.image.AxesImage at 0x257ac2d23d0>
```

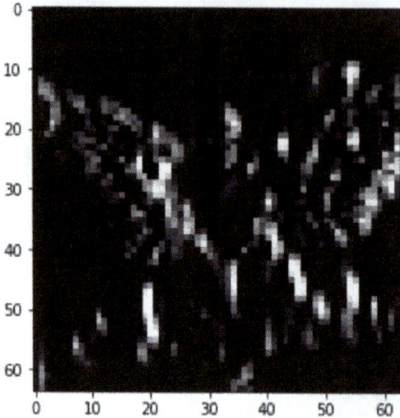

Example 2. Detecting vertical edges using 3x3 matrix M1.

```
horizontal = np.array([[1, 1, 1], [0, 0, 0], [-1, -1, -1]])
image_ver = cv2.filter2D(image,-1,horizontal)
imshow(image_ver)
```

```
<matplotlib.image.AxesImage at 0x257ac32c610>
```

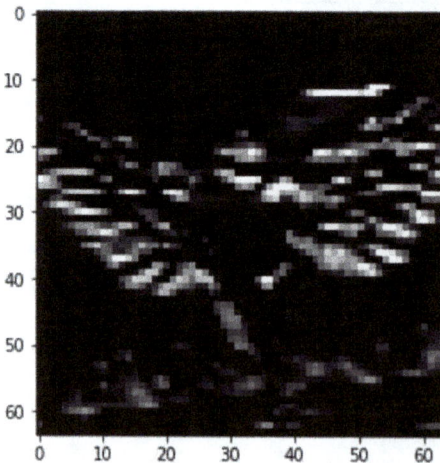

Example 3. Detecting Horizontal edges using 3x3 matrix M2.

Similar to the above process of edge extraction there are multiple ways for extracting important features of images in the dataset. These extracted features are further used to train the predicting model. Some of the important feature extraction algorithm are GLCM (Gray-Level Co-occurrence Matrix), LBP (Local Binary Pattern), (HoG) Histogram of Oriented Gradients, etc. Extracted features are given as input to train the model. However, feature extraction is a tedious task to perform and also require domain knowledge related to dataset for extracting relevant features. To efficiently train a model it is very much required to extract important information from the images and reduce the dimension of raw dataset. This process of selecting effective features is called feature extraction. Convolution operation has made a remarkable change in the era of neural network by automating the process of large number of feature extraction from the image dataset. In the upcoming topic we will discuss the process of convolution over a grey-scale image.

5.2. Convolution Over 2D Image/Array

Convolution is major part of any Convolutional Neural Network (CNN) used to extract valuable information or features from the image datasets. This process of extracting features of an image is done my convolving multiple kernels (small matrix) with different weights/values over an image. The elements-wise dot product is calculated between kernel values and the image values to give particular value of an output image. Similarly, kernel is shifted over an image to calculate another value of output image. This output image after the process of convolution is called a feature map. In this way, after convolving multiple kernels over a single image we get multiple feature maps as shown in Fig. 5.1. If 100 kernels are applied over an image than we would have 100 output features maps. These feature maps contain important information about the image, which is use to train the model for classification of particular image. As shown in the below figure, convolution is applied over an image of numeric 8 using 12 different kernels resulting 12 different feature maps. All 12 feature maps would be containing various information or features of the input image. For example, some of the feature maps may be containing edges information. Some other feature maps might be containing information about texture and so on.

Each feature map contains some important
Information or features of the input image.

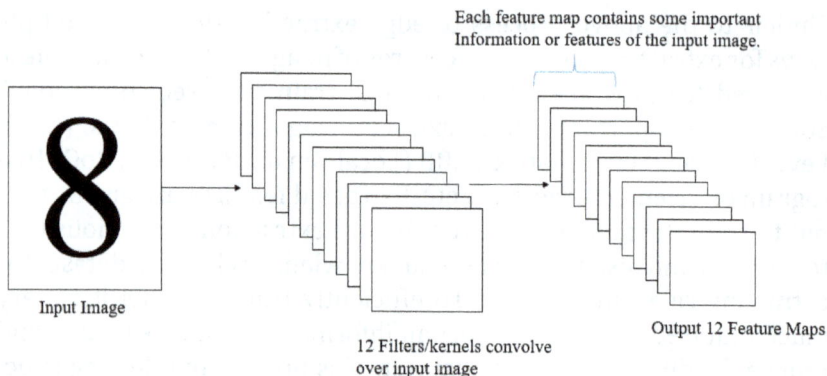

Input Image

Output 12 Feature Maps

12 Filters/kernels convolve
over input image

Fig. 5.1 Multiple kernels convolve over input image to give equal number of feature maps.

5.2.1 Convolution Process with Stride 1

Stride rate represent the speed of sliding kernel over an input matrix (or image). The process of convolution using 3x3 kernel with some weights over an array of 4x4 with stride 1 is shown in Fig. 5.2. **Stride 1** means that after calculating dot product of kernel over first 3x3 quadrant of input image, the kernel shift right by one column. Further, calculate the dot product for another quadrant of input image. After that, kernel shift towards down with one row to convolve the remaining quadrants of the input image.

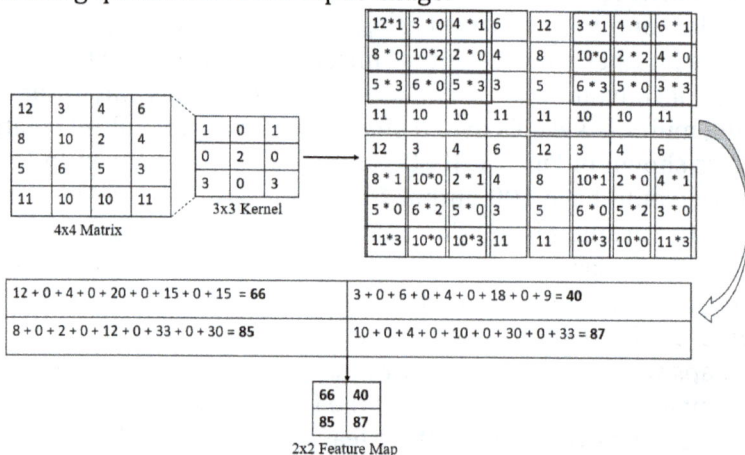

12	3	4	6
8	10	2	4
5	6	5	3
11	10	10	11

4x4 Matrix

1	0	1
0	2	0
3	0	3

3x3 Kernel

12*1	3 * 0	4 * 1	6	12	3 * 1	4 * 0	6 * 1
8 * 0	10*2	2 * 0	4	8	10*0	2 * 2	4 * 0
5 * 3	6 * 0	5 * 3	3	5	6 * 3	5 * 0	3 * 3
11	10	10	11	11	10	10	11
12	3	4	6	12	3	4	6
8 * 1	10*0	2 * 1	4	8	10*1	2 * 0	4 * 1
5 * 0	6 * 2	5 * 0	3	5	6 * 0	5 * 2	3 * 0
11*3	10*0	10*3	11	11	10*3	10*0	11*3

12 + 0 + 4 + 0 + 20 + 0 + 15 + 0 + 15 = 66	3 + 0 + 6 + 0 + 4 + 0 + 18 + 0 + 9 = 40
8 + 0 + 2 + 0 + 12 + 0 + 33 + 0 + 30 = 85	10 + 0 + 4 + 0 + 10 + 0 + 30 + 0 + 33 = 87

66	40
85	87

2x2 Feature Map

Fig. 5.2 Process of convolution with stride 1.

As per the Fig. 5.2 convolution of 3x3 kernel over an array (or portion of image) of 4x4 will give 2x2 feature map. However, if we further shift the kernel after second shift towards left than the kernel will go out of image. And we will not able to calculate the dot product of kernel and input array. Similarly, if we move the kernel downwards after second shift operation than also kernel reach out of the input matrix and dot product would not be possible as shown in Fig. 5.3 (a) and (b).

12	3	4 * 1	6 * 0	?*1
8	10	2 * 0	4 * 2	?*0
5	6	5 * 3	3 * 0	?*3
11	10	10	11	

(a)

12	3	4	6
8	10	2	4
5 * 1	6 * 0	5 * 1	3
11*0	10*2	10*0	11
?*3	?*0	?*3	

(b)

Fig. 5.3 Cannot process Convolution when (a) kernel get out of image after second shift (stride 1) towards right (b) kernel go out of image after second shift (stride 1) in downward direction.

5.2.2 Convolution Process with Stride 2

In case of convolution with stride 2, after calculating the dot product of first quadrant of an input image the kernel move towards right leaving two columns instead of one (as in case of stride 1). Then kernel do convolution over next portion of an image. Further, kernel move downwards leaving two rows to convolve the remaining image as shown in Fig. 5.4. In the below figure input matrix or portion of image is of size 4x4 and the kernel size used for convolution process is 2x2.

12*1	3 * 0	4	6		12	3	4 * 1	6 * 0
8 * 3	10*2	2	4		8	10	2 * 3	4 * 2
5	6	5	3		5	6	5	3
11	10	10	11		11	10	10	11

12	3	4	6
8	10	2	4
5	6	5	3
11	10	10	11

4x4 Matrix

| 1 | 0 |
| 3 | 2 |

2x2 Kernel

12	3	4	6		12	3	4	6
8	10	2	4		8	10	2	4
5 * 1	6 * 0	5	3		5	6	5 * 1	3 * 0
11*3	10*2	10	11		11	10	10*3	11*2

| 56 | 18 |
| 58 | 57 |

2x2 Feature Map

| 12 + 0 + 24 + 20 = 56 | 4 + 0 + 6 + 8 = 18 |
| 5 + 0 + 33 + 20 = 58 | 5 + 0 + 30 + 22 = 57 |

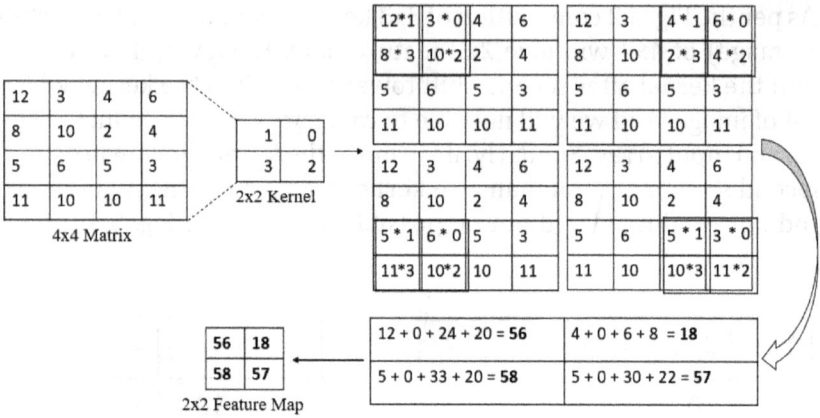

Fig. 5.4 Process of convolution with stride 2.

5.2.3 Padding

The main drawback of convolution is that with every convolution process the size of the matrix get reduced. Further, the ignorance of the border information of images. These drawbacks of the convolution process may result in loss of information. To overcome this problem we can use padding before convolution. Padding is the process of adding layers of 0s in the outer border of the image, to provide extra space for kernel to convolve over an image.

```python
import numpy as np
import tensorflow as tf
```

```python
m = np.array([[12, 3, 4, 6],
              [8, 10, 2, 4],
              [5, 6, 5, 3],
              [11, 10, 10, 11]])
print(m.dtype)
```

```
int32
```

```python
m = m.reshape(4, 4, 1)
m = m[None, :, :, :]
print(m.shape)
m = m.astype(float)
print(m.dtype)
```

```
(1, 4, 4, 1)
float64
```

```python
y = tf.keras.layers.Conv2D(filters = 1, kernel_size = (3,3),
                           strides = (1,1), padding = "valid",
                           input_shape=m.shape)(m)
```

```python
print((y[0,:,:,0]).shape)
```

```
(2, 2)
```

Example 4. The size of feature map get reduced to 2x2 from 4x4 (input matrix).

To understand the importance of padding, consider above Example 4, in which we have taken a 4x4 array 'm' and performed certain operations. Firstly, the array is reshaped m = m.reshape(4, 4, 1) to add information about the number of channels (1 in this case). Then we have increased the dimension of an array m = m[None, :, :, :] to provide information about the number of images (matrices) which is 0 in this case. Further, the matrix is converted into float64 (dtype = float) from int32 (dtype = integer). All the above operations are performed to process the convolution operation. As in 'Conv2D' function of KERAS API, it is required to provide the information about the number of images in the dataset and number of channels in each image. Therefore, matrix m is reshaped and incremented with one more dimension. Further, as the weights of kernels (filters) could be in floating point numbers also therefore, it is required to convert the matrix from integer to float before processing the convolution operation. Now we will discuss the parameters mentioned in 'Conv2D' function as shown below.

y = tf.keras.layers.Conv2D(filters = 1, kernel_size = (3,3), strides = (1,1), padding = "valid", input_shape=m.shape)(m)
filters = 1, number of kernels (filters) to be applied on the matrix.
kernel_size = (3,3), represent the size of kernel (filter) which is 3x3 in this case.

strides = (1,1), stide 1 is used (as discussed in 5.2.1 section).
padding = "valid", it means no padding is used.

input_shape=m.shape, providing the information about the shape of image (matrix).
(m), convolution is applied over matrix m.

In the last line, that is print((y[0,:,:,0]).shape) the shape of single feature map y[0, :, :, 0] created after convolution will be displayed. However, shape of feature map get reduced to 2x2 from 4x4. The size of feature map depends on the size of input matrix/image and the size of kernel used. The general formula for calculating the size of resultant feature map after performing convolution operation with stride = 1 is shown below in Eq. 1.

$$\textbf{nxn} * \textbf{fxf} = \textbf{(n – f + 1)x(n – f + 1)} \tag{1}$$

where,
nxn is the shape of input matrix.
fxf is kernel size, used for convolution process.
'*' used for representing the convolution.

For example, if n = 4 and f = 3 than the size of the resultant feature map will be n-f+1 therefore, the feature map would be of shape 2x2.

In order to overcome this drawback of information loss, padding is applied before convolution by changing the parameter padding = 'same' instead of 'valid'. When we choose the option padding = 'same', the input matrix gets padded with zeros as shown in Fig. 5.5 before convolution. After padding, the size of input matrix change from 4x4 to 6x6. Therefore, after applying convolution over padded matrix the resultant matrix (feature map) size remain equal to the input matrix. As shown in Example 5, by changing parameter padding = 'same' the shape of resultant feature map (4x4) remain same as shape of input matrix (4x4) after convolution process.

0	0	0	0	0	0
0	12	3	4	6	0
0	8	10	2	4	0
0	5	6	5	3	0
0	11	10	10	11	0
0	0	0	0	0	0

Fig. 5.5 Shape change from 4x4 to 6x6 after padding

With padding = 'same' the size of the resultant image after performing convolution operation with **stride = 1** is represented as shown in Eq. 2.

$$nxn * fxf = (n + 2p - f + 1)x(n + 2p - f + 1) \tag{2}$$

where, p is the padding size.

However, the question is how much padding is required to keep the size of feature map(output image after convolution with stride = 1) same as the size of input image? The general formula to calculate the required padding is shown below in Eq. 3.

$$n + 2p - f + 1 = n$$
$$2p - f + 1 = 0$$
$$p = (f - 1) / 2 \tag{3}$$

Example, if filter size is f = 3 than the required padding would be

⇨ $n + 2p - f + 1 = n$
⇨ $2p - f + 1 = 0$

⇨ $p = (f - 1) / 2$
⇨ $p = (3 - 1) / 2$
⇨ **p = 1**

Now putting value p = 1 in Eq. 2 for calculating the size of resultant image(feature map) if **n = 4**.

⇨ $(n + 2p - f + 1)x(n + 2p - f + 1)$
⇨ $(4 + 2*1 - 3 + 1)x(4 + 2*1 - 3 + 1)$
⇨ $(4 + 2 - 3 + 1)x(4 + 2 - 3 + 1)$
⇨ **4x4**

As we can see that the size of resultant matrix is same as the size of input matrix (n = 4).

The process of convolution with padding = 'same' is shown in below Example 5.

```python
import numpy as np
import tensorflow as tf
```

```python
m = np.array([[12, 3, 4, 6],
              [8, 10, 2, 4],
              [5, 6, 5, 3],
              [11, 10, 10, 11]])
```

```python
m = m.reshape(4, 4, 1)
m = m[None, :, :, :]
m = m.astype(float)
print(m.shape, m.dtype)
```

```
(1, 4, 4, 1) float64
```

```python
y = tf.keras.layers.Conv2D(filters = 1, kernel_size = (3,3),
                           strides = (1,1), padding = "same",
                           input_shape=m.shape)(m)
```

```python
print((y[0,:,:,0]).shape)
```

```
(4, 4)
```

Example 5. The size of feature map (4x4) remain same as input matrix (4x4) after applying convolution using kernel of size 3x3 with padding = 'same' and stride = 1.

The general formula for representing the resultant matrix/image after performing the convolution operation over a matrix of size n using **stride > 1** with filter size f is shown in Eq. 4.

$$nxn * fxf = floor[(n + 2p - f) / s + 1] \times floor[(n + 2p - f) / s + 1] \quad (4)$$

Where,
nxn is size of input matrix.
fxf is filter(kernel) size.
p is padding.
s is stride.
'*' represents the convolution operation.
floor is representing the floor value of any fractional value eg. Floor[3.45] = 3.

For example, considering n = 7, f = 3, p = 0 (padding = 'valid') and s = 2 than the size of resultant image (according to Eq. 4.) after performing convolution operation would be as shown below.

⇨ 7x7 * 3x3 = floor[((7 + 2.0 − 3) / 2) + 1)] x floor[((7 + 2.0 − 3) / 2) + 1)]

⇨ 7x7 * 3x3 = floor[((7 + 0 − 3) / 2) + 1)] x floor[((7 + 0 − 3) / 2) + 1)]

⇨ 7x7 * 3x3 = 3x3

We can verify the above example by implementing in python as shown below (Example 6.)

```
import numpy as np
import tensorflow as tf
```

```
m = np.random.randint(10, size=(7, 7))
```

```
m = m.reshape(7, 7, 1)
m = m[None, :, :, :]
m = m.astype(float)
print(m.shape, m.dtype)
```

```
(1, 7, 7, 1) float64
```

```
y = tf.keras.layers.Conv2D(filters = 1, kernel_size = (3,3),
                           strides = (2,2), padding = "valid",
                           input_shape=m.shape)(m)
```

```
print((y[0,:,:,0]).shape)
```

```
(3, 3)
```

Example 6. The size of the resultant feature map is 3x3 after applying convolution over input matrix n = 7 using f = 3, padding = 'valid', and stride = 2.

The above example is almost the same as example 5. However, the only difference is in Example 6 a random matrix 'm' is generated using randint() function instead of a matrix with user-defined values.

All elements of matrix 'm' are restricted with in range 0 to 10.
For a better understanding of the randint() method, let's take one more example in which 25 random integer numbers are generated with in the range of 0 to 10 as shown in Example 7.

```
import numpy as np
```

```
m = np.random.randint(10, size = (5,5))
```

```
print(m)
```

```
[[4 2 4 8 8]
 [1 2 7 4 0]
 [1 8 0 3 9]
 [6 9 7 0 3]
 [7 1 5 2 7]]
```

Example 7. Generation random numpy array of size 7x7 using rand-int function.

5.2.4 Implementation of Convolution over Grey-scale Image Using Python

In this section, we will implement the process of convolution with different number of kernels over the grey-scale image as shown in Example 9 and visualize the output feature maps. Grey-scale images are basically a 2D matrix in which all pixels values are with in range of 0 to 255 as shown in Example 8. Further the shape of the grey-scale image is the size of 2D matrix. Therefore, any grey-scale image can be easily represented as a numpy integer array and multiple operations can be performed over it.

```
import cv2
from skimage.io import imshow
```

```
image = cv2.imread("meandkunkun.jpeg",0)
imshow(image)
print(image.shape)
```

(1152, 864)

```
print(image)
```

```
[[ 34  34  34 ...  52  51  51]
 [ 33  33  33 ...  52  51  51]
 [ 31  31  31 ...  52  51  51]
 ...
 [135 136 137 ... 171 170 170]
 [134 135 137 ... 163 162 162]
 [133 134 137 ... 156 156 155]]
```

```
print(image.dtype)
```

```
uint8
```

Example. 8. Image represented as numpy integer array with values in range (0-255).

Now let us see how we can perform convolution operation over a grey-scale image. For convolution 'Conv2D' function has been used which is provided by keras API.

```python
import cv2
from skimage.io import imshow
import tensorflow as tf
import matplotlib.pyplot as plt
```

```python
image = cv2.imread("meandkunkun.jpeg",0)
image = cv2.resize(image,(64, 64))
imshow(image)
```

```
<matplotlib.image.AxesImage at 0x1ef447e9e80>
```

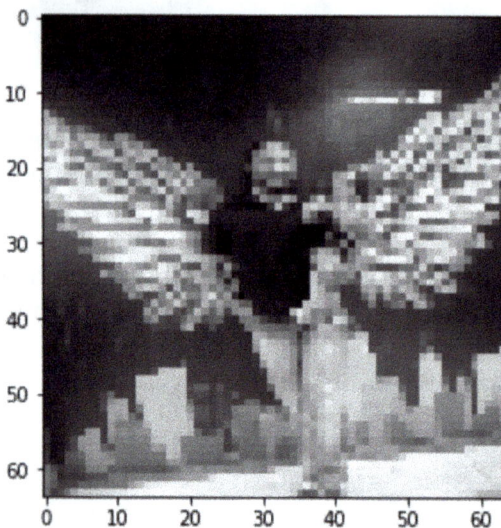

```python
img1 = image.reshape(64,64,1)
img1 = img1[None, :, :, :]
img1 = img1.astype(float)
print(img1.shape)
```

```
(1, 64, 64, 1)
```

```python
y = tf.keras.layers.Conv2D(5, (3,3), strides = (1,1),
                           padding = "same", activation = 'relu',
                           input_shape=img1.shape)(img1)
```

```python
print(y.shape)
```

```
(1, 64, 64, 5)
```

```
plt.imshow(y[0, :, :, 0])
```

```
<matplotlib.image.AxesImage at 0x1ef44072490>
```

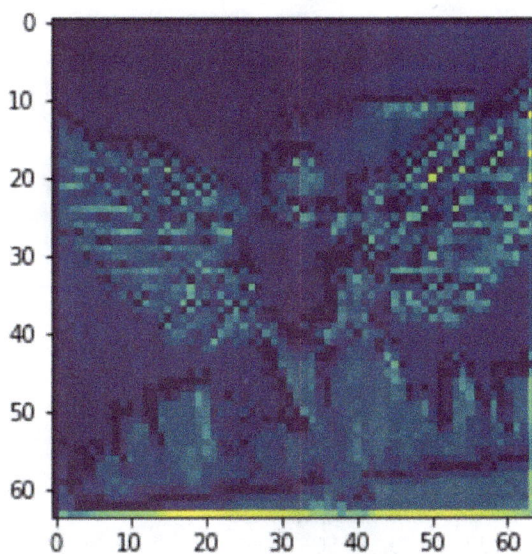

```
plt.imshow(y[0, :, :, 1])
```

```
<matplotlib.image.AxesImage at 0x1ef441f91c0>
```

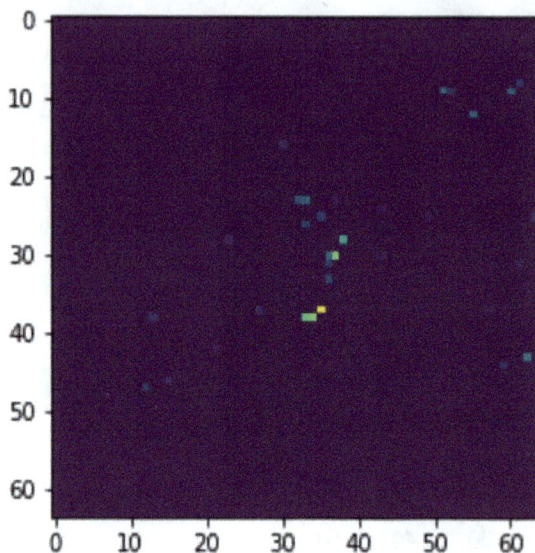

```
plt.imshow(y[0, :, :, 2])
```

```
<matplotlib.image.AxesImage at 0x1ef458f9280>
```

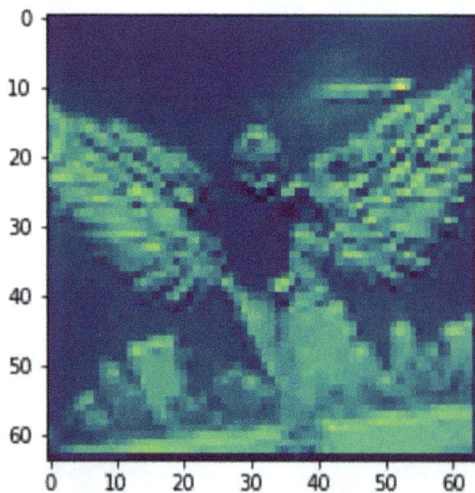

```
plt.imshow(y[0, :, :, 3])
```

```
<matplotlib.image.AxesImage at 0x1ef459533a0>
```

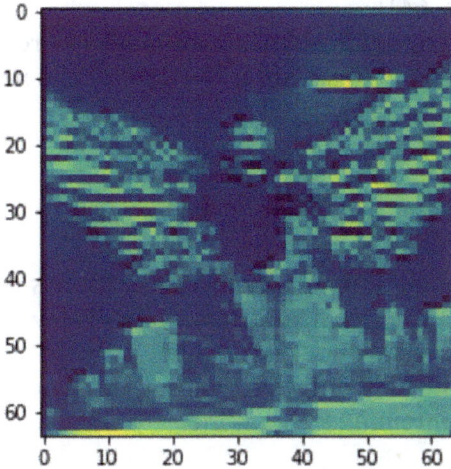

```
plt.imshow(y[0, :, :, 4])
```

```
<matplotlib.image.AxesImage at 0x1ef459ad730>
```

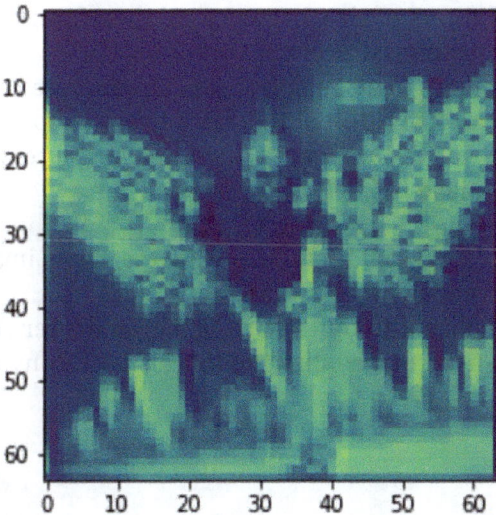

Example 9. Implementation of convolution operation using 5 kernels (filters) of size 3x3.

In above Example 9, a color image converted into grey-scale image by incorporating 0 in imread() function of cv2 library
image = cv2.imread("meandkunkun.jpeg", 0).
Further, image resized to 64x64 using resize() function
image = cv2.resize(image,(64, 64)).
Input image further reshaped by adding two more dimensions representing the number of images (1 in this case) in the dataset and number of channels (1 in this case) in each image.
img1 = image.reshape(64,64,1)
img1 = img1[None, :, :, :]
img1 = img1.astype(float)

After above pre-processing of input image, 'Conv2D' function is used for convolution with 5 filters each of size 3x3 as shown below. All parameters in the below function are almost the same as discussed in the above topics. However, the only difference is the use of the activation function 'ReLU' for maintaining the non-linearity in the feature map.

```
y = tf.keras.layers.Conv2D(5, (3,3), strides = (1,1),
            padding = "same", activation = 'relu',
        input_shape=img1.shape)(img1)
```

As in 'Conv2D' function 5 filters of size 3x3 are used therefore, 5 different channels would be generated after convolution. That is, a stack or volume of 5 different images (feature maps) will be generated corresponding to the convolution of 5 different kernels over an input image. The padding = 'same' so, the size of resultant image will remain same as the size of input image (64, 64).

print(y.shape) will show (1, 64, 64, 5) as output that is single image of size 64x64 with 5 different channels from index 0 to 4.
We can use slicing to visualize different images generated after convolution. Following lines used to visualize the images with convolution of different kernels.
plt.imshow(y[0, :, :, 0])
plt.imshow(y[0, :, :, 1])
plt.imshow(y[0, :, :, 2])
plt.imshow(y[0, :, :, 3])
plt.imshow(y[0, :, :, 4])

5.3 Convolution Over Color Image (3D)

As compared to any grey-scale image, color images have 3 channels instead of 1. Each channel represents the color in form of **R**ed, **G**reen and **B**lue that is RGB as shown in Example 10. In the example, color image read as grey-scale and color as well. In case of grey-scale image, the shape of image is not showing any separate dimension for representing channel. That is the shape of grey-scale image is just showing the size of image in row, columns. However, in case of color image the shape attribute has shown additional dimension representing the number of channels (3 in this case). Each channel is 2D matrix with different pixel values (in range of 0-255) representing the contribution of red, green and blue color (RGB) in the image.

```python
import cv2
from skimage.io import imshow
```

```python
image_rgb = cv2.imread("meandkunkun.jpeg")
image_gs = cv2.imread("meandkunkun.jpeg", 0)
```

```python
imshow(image_gs)
print(image_gs.shape)
```

```
(1152, 864)
```

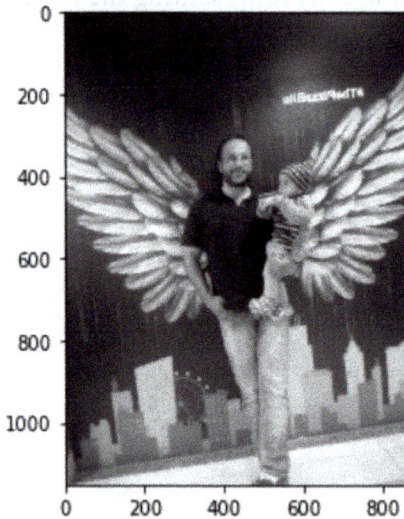

```
imshow(image_rgb)
print(image_rgb.shape)
```

```
(1152, 864, 3)
```

Example 10. Grey-image 2D whereas color image 3D (volume of three images (RGB)).

During the convolution over 3D image or volume of images, the number of channels in the kernel should be equal to the number of channels in the input image as shown in Fig. 5.6.

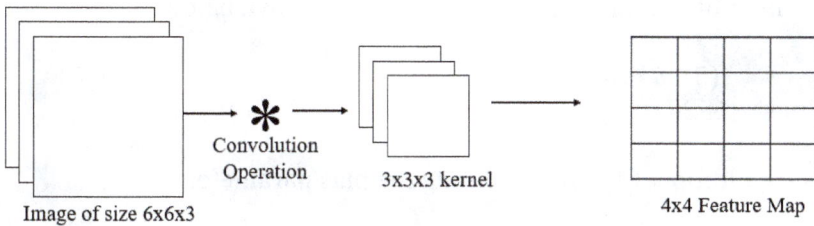

Fig. 5.6 Number of channels in the image and kernel should be equal.

Further, number of feature maps extracted from input 3D image is always equal to the number of 3D kernels convolve over an image. As shown in Fig. 5.7, two volume kernels applied over a volume image to extract feature maps with local information of vertical and horizontal edges.

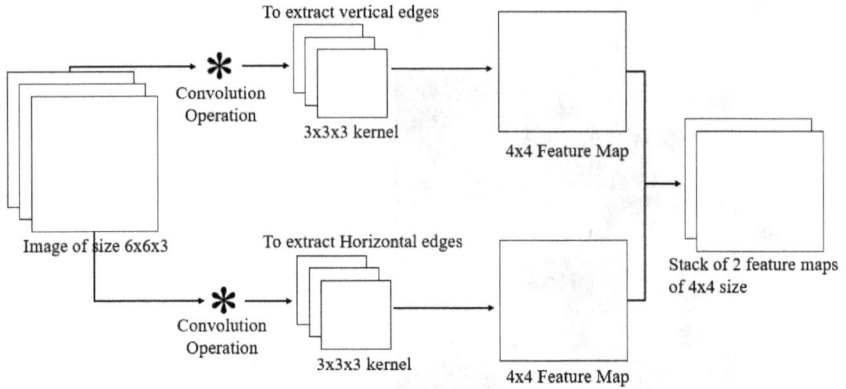

Fig. 5.7 Number of feature maps are always equal to the number of kernels applied in the process of convolution.

The values in each kernel known as parameters, these parameters used to find the number of features in an image. In next section, we will see how to calculate total number of parameters.

5.4 Number of Parameters Used to Extract Image Features

Total number of parameters are equal to the number of values in one kernel and bias value (any real number) multiplied with total number of kernels. If we have 20 kernels and each of size 5x5x3, than the total number of parameters would be 1520 as shown below.

⇨ [(5 * 5 * 3) + 1] * 20
⇨ 1520

Here additional 1 is representing the bias parameter.

These parameters used to find number of features in an image. Further, the number of parameters are always remain same independent from the size of input image. Complete convolution process can be represented as shown in Fig. 5.8.

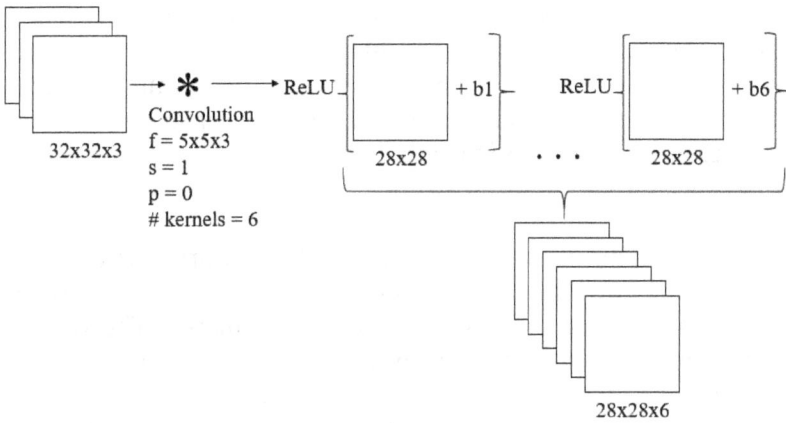

Fig. 5.8 Representing complete one convolution process.

In the above figure, input image is of size 32x32x3 and 6 filters each of size 5x5x3 are convolve over input image. The size of the output feature maps would be 28x28 as per Eq. 4, calculated below.

⇨ 32x32 * 3x3 = floor[((n + 2p – f) / s) + 1]x floor[((n + 2p – f) / s) + 1]

⇨ 32x32 * 3x3 = floor[((32 + 0 – 5) / 1) + 1]x floor[((32 + 0 – 5) / 1) + 1]

⇨ 32x32 * 3x3 = floor[27 + 1]x floor[27 + 1]

⇨ 32x32 * 3x3 = 28x28 (feature map)

In each feature map, one extra parameter is add called bias. Bias can be any real number (mostly 1), bias in the above figure represented by b1, b2...b6. Further activation function ReLU applied to each feature map to reduce the linearity generated after convolution process. The total number of feature maps would be 6 therefore, the size of resultant volume after convolution process will be 28x28x6. That is, 6 feature maps and each of size 28x28.

Summary

Convolution is the process of convolving multiple filters over an image (matrix) to extract various features of the image. Feature extraction is tedious task and require domain knowledge. As it is not feasible to consider each pixel value of the image as a feature of image.

Therefore, it is required to extract some important features from an image and use these features to train the model. Convolution process has automate the process of feature extraction using multiple kernels. Kernels are small (generally 3x3) matrices with certain values use for the process of convolution to extract important information from image dataset.

Convolution of kernel over an image result a feature map of reduced dimension. In convolution, dot product of kernel values and the values of image under the kernel matrix is calculated. The recursive computation of the dot product gives the resultant feature map. Each kernel gives a separate feature map with some important information about the image. If we convolve 100 kernels over an image then it will result 100 feature maps containing information about an image.

In stride rate of 1, kernel convolve over input image by shifting single step at a time. In case of stride 2, kernel shift with two steps after each convolution. The major drawbacks of convolution process is ignorance of border information of images and reduced dimension of feature maps. Padding used to minimize these drawbacks of convolution process. In padding, layers of 0s are added in the outer border of the input matrix before convolution process. Through padding we can get resultant feature maps of same dimension as the input image.

Questions

1. What is the drawback of considering pixel value of an image as a feature of image?
2. What do you understand by the term stride rate in convolution? Explain with the help of example.
3. Comment on the statement "convolution process ignore the border information of input image."
4. WAP in python to extract horizontal and vertical edges of an image and display the resultants images with edges information on the console.
5. WAP in python to apply convolution using 3x3 kernel over 5x5 matrix with random values within range of 0 – 9. In addition, explain the effect of convolution on the dimension of input matrix.

6. *WAP in python to apply convolution process on color image using 5 kernels with padding and display all the resultant feature maps.
7. WAP in python to explain the role of padding in the process of convolution.
8. Calculate the size of feature map, if 3x3 kernel convolve over 5x5 input matrix without padding with stride = 1.
9. Recalculate the size of feature map for question 7 with padding.
10. If the input color image is of size 100x100x3 and 5 kernels each of size 3x3x3 are used for convolution process. Then calculate the total number of parameters used for feature extraction.

Solutions:

Question 6

```python
import cv2
from skimage.io import imshow
import matplotlib.pyplot as plt
import tensorflow as tf
```

```python
image = cv2.imread("meandkunkun.jpeg")
imshow(image)
print(image.shape)
```

```
(1152, 864, 3)
```

```
print(image.dtype)
```

```
uint8
```

```
print(image.shape)
```

```
(1152, 864, 3)
```

```
img1 = image[None, :, :, :]
```

```
print(img1.shape)
```

```
(1, 1152, 864, 3)
```

```
img1 = img1.astype(float)
```

```
y = tf.keras.layers.Conv2D(5, (3,3), strides = (1,1),
                           padding = "same", activation = 'relu',
                           input_shape=img1.shape)(img1)
```

```
print(y.shape)
```

```
(1, 1152, 864, 5)
```

```
plt.imshow(y[0, :, :, 0])
```

```
<matplotlib.image.AxesImage at 0x247be99d430>
```

```
plt.imshow(y[0, :, :, 1])
```

<matplotlib.image.AxesImage at 0x247be9f64c0>

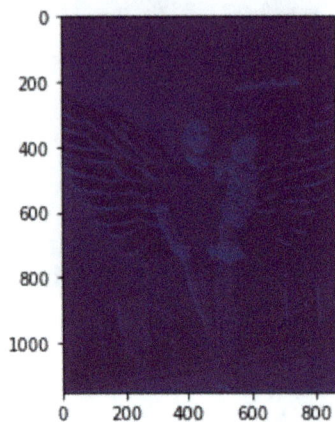

```
plt.imshow(y[0, :, :, 2])
```

<matplotlib.image.AxesImage at 0x247bea514f0>

```
plt.imshow(y[0, :, :, 3])
```

```
<matplotlib.image.AxesImage at 0x247beaab520>
```

```
plt.imshow(y[0, :, :, 4])
```

```
<matplotlib.image.AxesImage at 0x247beb06580>
```

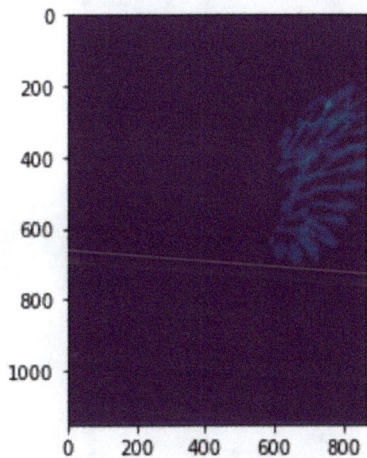

6

Activation Functions

Activation function also known as transfer function. It transform the weighted sum of the inputs of the node into the output of that node. The output further passed as input to other connected nodes. The major purpose of activation function is to add non-linearity to the neural network model, to make it robust for the accurate prediction of unknown test cases. Activation function can be broadly classify into two types that is linear and non-linear. Linear activation function is straight-line function where output is proportional to the input. Therefore, non-linear activation function are mostly used in neural network model. In this chapter, non-linear activation functions are discussed with their implementation in python programming language.

6.1 Brief Introduction to Neural Network and Activation Function

Before discussing about the purpose and working of activation function, it is essential to know about the basic working of neural network. Considering a small neural network with one input, one hidden and one output layer as shown in Fig 6.1.

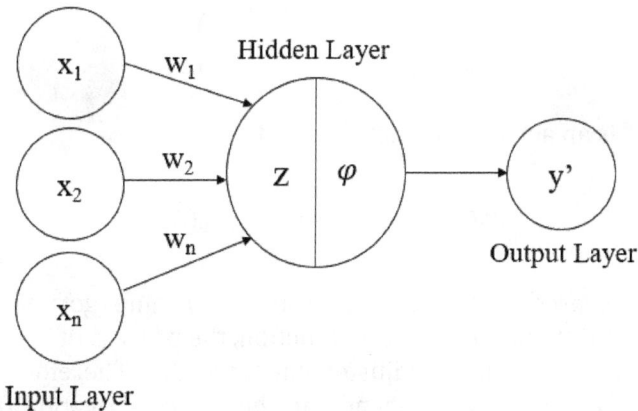

Fig. 6.1 Simple neural network.

The input layer in the neural network contains the neurons (nodes) equal to the number of features in the table (dataset). The values of these features (row in table) given as input to the input layer. One value to each neuron of input layer. Weights are assigned to each edge connecting the neurons of input and hidden layers as mention in the above figure. Neuron (one in this case) of the hidden layer receives the summation of product of feature values and weights assigned to corresponding edges which is represented by 'z'. Activation function (mathematical function) applied to the value of 'z' and result (y') pass to the output layer. This y' is a hypothetical results received because of input features, assigned weights and some mathematical functions. Further, the value of y' compared with the corresponding ground truth value (dependent variable) under column y for the particular input features. Now the difference between y and y' calculated using Eq. 3, which is considered as loss (C). If the loss is high than we back-propagate the network to adjust the weights and recalculate the loss. This recursive process continues until loss minimized to a certain calibrated threshold value.

The value of 'z' and 'φ' can be calculated using Eq. (1) and (2) respectively.

$$z = \sum_{i=1}^{n} (w_i * x_i) + w_0 * b \ (1)$$

Where, b is bias which could be any natural number in most of the cases bias considered as 1.

$$\varphi = f(z) \qquad (2)$$

Where, f is an activation function.

$$C = \frac{1}{2}(y' - y)^2 \qquad (3)$$

Where, y' is predicted value and y is an actual value (gorund truth). Based on the result of activation function, the process of back-propagation carried out for the adjustement of weights. Therefore, efficent learing of model widely depends on the choice activation function. Activation function are used in hidden and output layer only.

Activation function play a vital role in the training of any neural network based model. It decides the contribution of a perticular neuron in making an appropriate hypothesis. Further, activation function introduce non-linearity in the model to make it robust and also reduces the chance of overfitting. By the term robust, means that the model should be capable to give good results for unseen inputs. Further, overfitting means that the model can perform well only for the seen inputs but lose its capability for unseen inputs. The decision boundary for good fit and over fit is shown in Fig. 6.2.

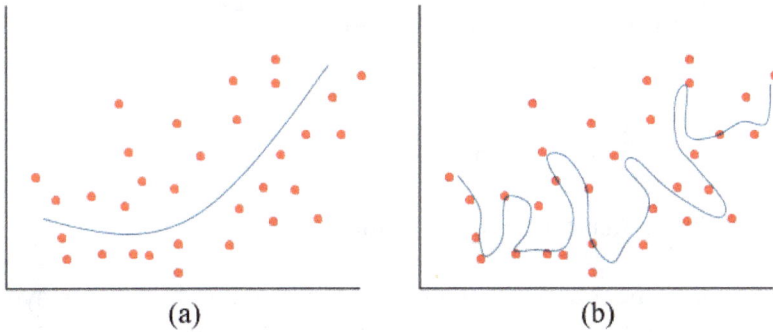

Fig. 6.2. (a) Good Fit (b) Over Fit

6.2 Activation Function for Hidden Layers

Hidden layers are the layers between input and output layer in the neural network model. Hidden layers accept input from the previous layer which could be a hidden or input layer, and gives output to another hidden layer or output layer as shown in Fig 6.3. There could be any number of hidden layers in the nework according to the application.

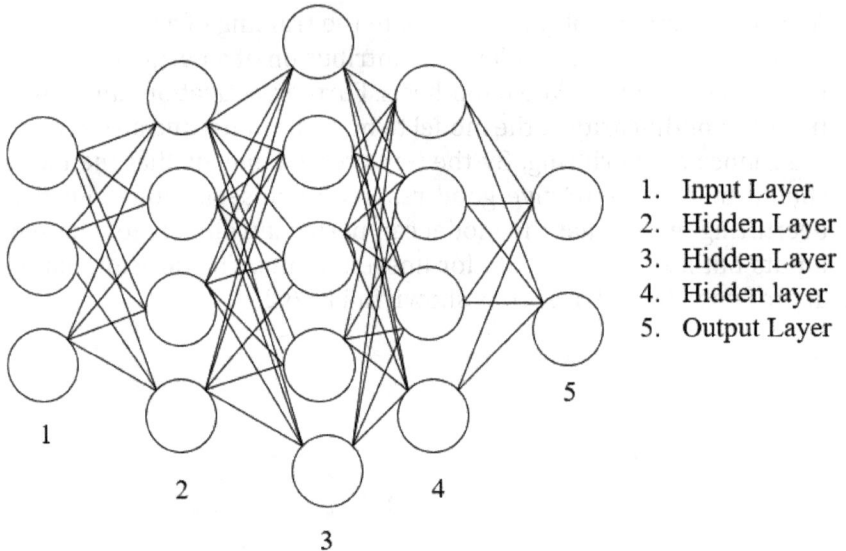

Fig. 6.3 Neural network with three hidden layers.

1. Input Layer
2. Hidden Layer
3. Hidden Layer
4. Hidden layer
5. Output Layer

Mostly, non-linear activation functions are used in the hidden layers to provide the non-linearity to the model to make it robust. So, that the model perform well for unseen inputs also. Some the activation functions used in the hidden layers are disscused below.

6.2.1 Rectified Linear Activation (ReLU) - ReLU is most commonly used activation function in the hidden layers of a neural network-based model. Although ReLU gives an impression of a linear function. However, it reduces the linearity which may be introduced due to the convolution process. ReLU is both simple to implement (Eq. (4)) and effective as compared to other activation functions. It just returns 0 for any negative input as shown in Fig. 6.4. ReLU propagates only the positive input(z) to another hidden or output layer.

$$f(z) = \max(0, z) \qquad (4)$$

Where, input (z) is calculated using Eq. (1).

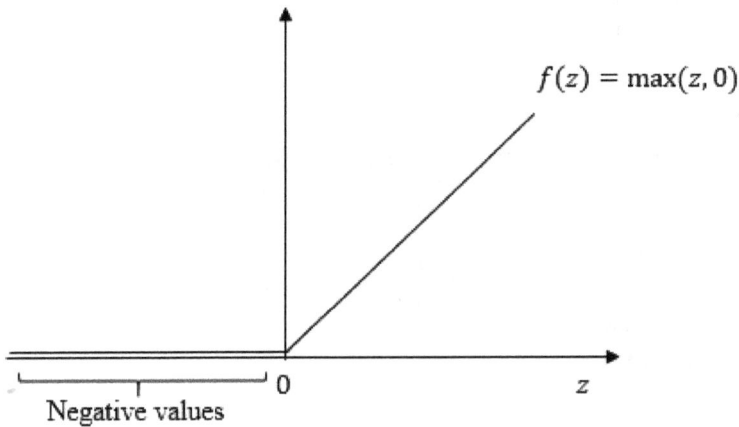

Fig. 6.4 Plot for ReLU activation function.

Now we will implement the ReLU activation function using python as shown in Example 1. Numpy and matplotlib libraries are imported to create a numpy array and plotting a graph. An array 'a' is taken as an input elements with in range of -8 to 8 with difference of 1.
a = np.array(range(-8, 8))

Now array 'a' will be having 16 elements. Further, an empty list a1 = [ ] is created to store the output values return by the user define function relu().
def relu(i):
  if i<0:
    return 0
  else:
    return i

This user-defined funtion accept one value at a time from the array 'a' and return 0 for every negative value. Further, the values return by the relu() functions are appended in the list 'a1' as output.
for i in a:
  a1.append(relu(i))
print(a1)

We can plot the graph between the input and the output values using matplotlib.
plt.plot(a, a1)

The complete implementation of ReLU activation function is shown below in Example 1.

```python
import numpy as np
from matplotlib import pyplot as plt
```

```python
a = np.array(range(-8, 8))
a1 = []
def relu(i):
    if i<0:
        return 0
    else:
        return i
for i in a:
    a1.append(relu(i))
print(a1)
```

```
[0, 0, 0, 0, 0, 0, 0, 0, 0, 1, 2, 3, 4, 5, 6, 7]
```

```python
plt.plot(a, a1)
```

```
[<matplotlib.lines.Line2D at 0x2ceca1e3670>]
```

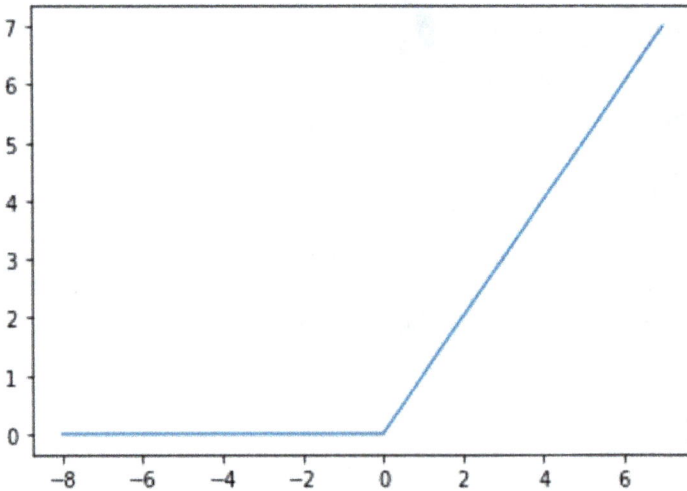

Example 1. Implementation fo ReLU activation function.

6.2.2 Sigmoid Activation Function – It takes any real value as an input and return output with in the range of 0 to 1. It is also known as logistic function. Sigmoid function gives output close to 1 for large positive input values where as, close to 0 for large negative inputs. This activation function can be used in both hidden and output layer. Its working is based on Eq. 5 and graphical representation is shown in Fig 6.5.

$$f(z) = \frac{1}{1 + e^{-z}} \qquad (5)$$

Where, input (z) is calculated using Eq. (1).

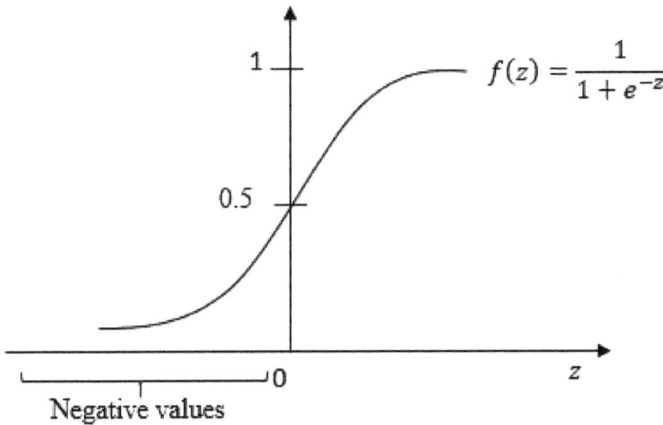

Fig. 6.5 Graphical representation of Sigmoid function.

Now we will implement the sigmoid activation function using python programming language as shown in Example 2. Here math library is imported for exponential function. The line by line explenation of the implementation is almost same as discussed in the previous topic. The only difference in the user-define function sigmoid(). Where all the input values are put in Eq. 5 and result is return by the function as an output.

```
def sigmoid(i):
    return 1/(1+exp(-i))
```

The output of sigmoid() function is appended in the list 'a1'.

```python
import numpy as np
from matplotlib import pyplot as plt
from math import exp
```

```python
a = np.array(range(-8, 8))
a1 = []
def sigmoid(i):
    return 1/(1+exp(-i))
for i in a:
    a1.append(sigmoid(i))
```

```python
plt.plot(a, a1)
```

```
[<matplotlib.lines.Line2D at 0x2ceca2a6970>]
```

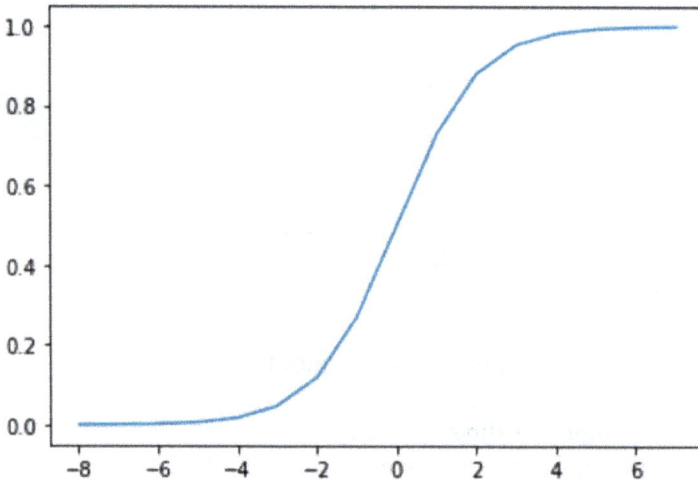

Example 2. Implementation of sigmpoid activation function.

6.2.3 Hyperbolic Tangent Activation Function – Tangent hyperbolic function also known as Tanh function. This activation function is very similar to the sigmoid function, moreover generate similar s-shaped curve. The only difference is that, this function takes any real value and generates the output within the range of -1 to 1 instead of 0 to 1 as in case of sigmoid function. Tanh function return output close to 1 for large positive values and give output close to -1 for large negative values. Eq. 6 represents the mathematical equation for Tanh function.

$$f(x) = \frac{1 - e^{-2x}}{1 + e^{-2x}} \qquad (6)$$

The graphical representation of Tanh function is shown in Fig. 6.6.

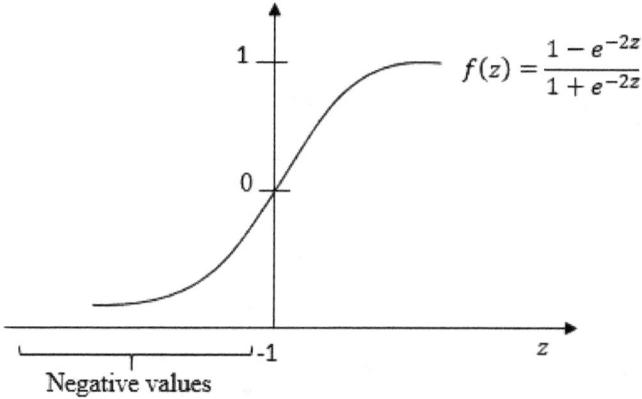

Fig. 6.6 Graph of Tanh activation function.

Implementation of the Tanh function using python is shown in Example 3.

```
a = np.array(range(-8, 8))
a1 = []
def Tanh(i):
    return (1-exp(-2*i))/(1+exp(-2*i))
for i in a:
    a1.append(Tanh(i))
```

```
plt.plot(a, a1)
```

```
[<matplotlib.lines.Line2D at 0x2ceca0e7550>]
```

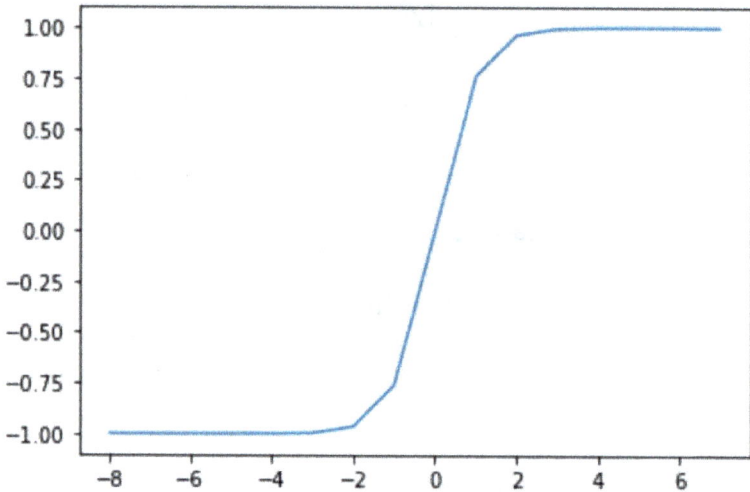

Example 3. Implementation of Tanh function.

6.3 Activation Function for Output Layers

Output layer provides the predicted output by the neural network. For binary classification, output layer can have one or two neurons. However, for multiple classification output layer should have neuron equal to the number of classes specified in the dataset. For example, if the network is trained for the classification of numerics from 0 to 9 then its output layer will have 10 neurons. Most commonly, two activation functions are used in neural network-based models that are sigmoid and softmax. Sigmoid activation function are used in binary classification and softmax function is used for the classification of multiple classes. Sigmoid function is already discussed in the previous section as it is also used in the hidden layers. Therefore, in this section we will discuss softmax activation function.

6.3.1 Softmax Activation Function – This function returns a vector with the classification probabilities of all the classes in the dataset in such a way that the sum of vector is always 1. The mathematical formula used to calculate the output of softmax activation function is show in Eq. 7.

$$f(z) = \frac{e^z}{sum\ (e^z)} \qquad (7)$$

Implementation of softmax function using python shown in Example 4. In which an array 'a' with five elements is taken as an input a = [1, 2, 5, 7]. The user-defined softmax function return the probability for each corresponding element in the input array 'a'.
def softmax(a):
  return exp(a) / exp(a).sum()

```
from numpy import exp
def softmax(x):
    return exp(x) / exp(x).sum()

a = [1, 2, 5, 7]
a1 = softmax(a)
print(a1)
print(a1.sum())
```

```
[0.0021657  0.00588697 0.11824302 0.87370431]
1.0
```

Example 4. Implementation of softmax activation function.

Summary

Activation functions are used in hidden and output layer of neural network based model. Activation function mathematically transform the inputs received by a neuron into a certain output, which is given as input to neurons of another connected layer. Mainly non-linear activation functions are used in neural network models to provide the non-linearity in the model for better performance. Moreover, minimize the problem of overfitting. Overfitting is the problem that arise when model respond well for the training data but show poor performance for unknown data. Overfitting can occur due to small training data.

ReLU is the most common activation function used in the hidden layer of the model. ReLU provides linearity to the model by passing all the positive inputs as it is and non-linearity by transforming all the negative values to zero. The linearity in the model enhances the speed of computation, whereas non-linearity makes the model robust.

Sigmoid activation function is mainly used in output layer of the model, it converts the real number within the range of 0 to 1. The output of the sigmoid activation function act as the probability of the hypothesis (prediction). The more the output value closer to one, the stronger the predicted result. Hyperbolic tangent activation function (tanh) is also very similar to the sigmoid activation function. The only difference is, tanh activation function takes any real number as an input and return the output within the range of -1 to 1 instead of 0 to 1.

Softmax activation functions are generally used in output layer, in multi-class classification problems. Whereas, sigmoid activation function used in case of binary classification models. Softmax activation function return the vector of probabilities representing the hypothesis (predicted value) for each class.

Questions

1. What do you understand by activation function? Explain its importance in the neural network model.
2. *WAP in python to apply ReLU activation function on a given array a1 = [-5, -4, -3, -2, -1, 0, 1, 2, 3, 4, 5] and return the list of output for given array a1. Also plot the graph for the same.
3. Why sigmoid activation function mainly used in the output layer of the neural network model.

4. What is the difference between sigmoid and tanh activation function?
5. *WAP in python to transform the array a1 (as mention in Question 2) using tanh activation function and plot the graph.
6. Explain the problem of overfitting.
7. *What are hyper parameters in the neural network model?
8. Explain softmax activation function.

Solutions:

Question 2

```python
import numpy as np
from matplotlib import pyplot as plt

a1 = np.array([-5, -4, -3, -2, -1, 0, 1, 2, 3, 4, 5])
a2 = []
def relu(i):
    if i<0:
        return 0
    else:
        return i
for i in a1:
    a2.append(relu(i))
print(a2)
```

```
[0, 0, 0, 0, 0, 0, 1, 2, 3, 4, 5]
```

```
plt.plot(a1, a2)
```

```
[<matplotlib.lines.Line2D at 0x272b5e365e0>]
```

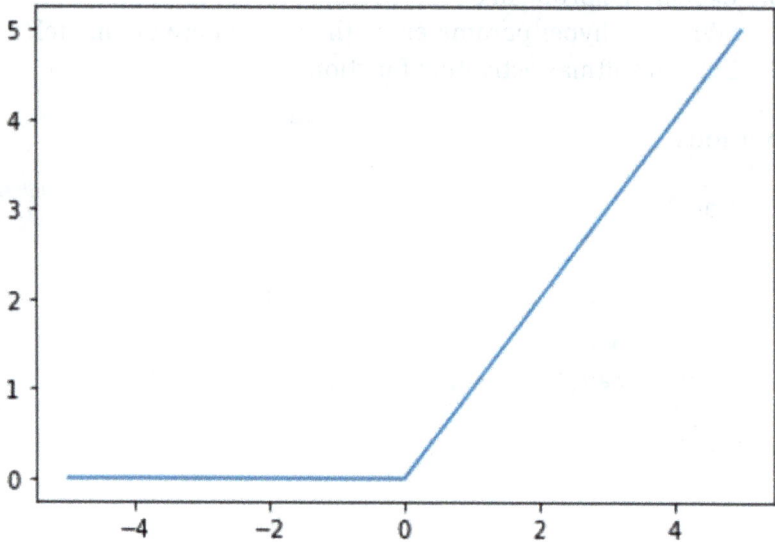

Question 5

```
import numpy as np
from matplotlib import pyplot as plt
from math import exp
```

```
a1 = np.array([-5, -4, -3, -2, -1, 0, 1, 2, 3, 4, 5])
a2 = []
def sigmoid(i):
    return 1/(1+exp(-i))
for i in a1:
    a2.append(sigmoid(i))
```

```
plt.plot(a1, a2)
```

```
[<matplotlib.lines.Line2D at 0x272b5e87a30>]
```

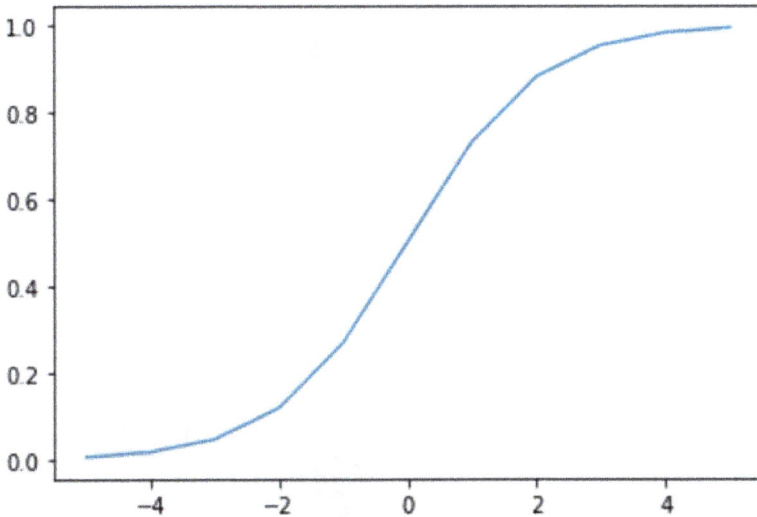

Question 7

Hyper-parameters are the variables that are set before the training of the model. These parameters are used to determine the structure of the network like the number of hidden layers in the model. Further, hyper-parameters also determine the training process of the model like the learning rate.

7

Pooling

Pooling layer is generally added after convolution and activation layer in Convolutional Neural Network (CNN). It is the process of sliding filter over feature map to summarize the features. Pooling is applied to each feature map and generate equal number of new set of features maps with reduced dimension. It can be broadly classified in two types max pooling and average pooling. In this chapter, we will discuss max pooling, average pooling, role of stride in pooling, and implementation of pooling operation over numpy array and image using keras.

7.1 Max Pooling

Max pooling is the process of sliding a filter generally of size 2x2 over feature map. Further, accessing the maximum number out of numbers under the filter. The speed of convolving filter depends on the stride rate. Stride = 1, means that filter start max-pooling process from upper left most part of the input feature map. After that, filter move ahead to next column to max-pool the numbers under the filter. Similarly, in downward direction filter move one row down to next row. The process of max-pooling is shown in Fig. 7.1. and Fig. 7.2. Recursive process of max-pooling over input feature map gives a down-sampled max-pooled feature map as show in Fig. 7.3.

1	2	3	4	5
2	3	3	5	6
1	1	1	1	2
4	4	5	6	7
5	4	4	4	3

Max(1, 2, 2, 3)

Max(2, 3, 3, 3)

Max(4, 5, 5, 6)

3	3	5	6

Max(3, 4, 3, 5)

1	2	3	4	5
2	3	3	5	6
1	1	1	1	2
4	4	5	6	7
5	4	4	4	3

1	2	3	4	5
2	3	3	5	6
1	1	1	1	2
4	4	5	6	7
5	4	4	4	3

1	2	3	4	5
2	3	3	5	6
1	1	1	1	2
4	4	5	6	7
5	4	4	4	3

Fig 7.1 Max-pooling performed on first row of the matrix with stride rate of 1.

1	2	3	4	5
2	3	3	5	6
1	1	1	1	2
4	4	5	6	7
5	4	4	4	3

Max(2, 3, 1, 1)

Max(3, 3, 1, 1)

3	3	5	6
3	3	5	6

Max(3, 5, 1, 1)

Max(5, 6, 1, 2)

1	2	3	4	5
2	3	3	5	6
1	1	1	1	2
4	4	5	6	7
5	4	4	4	3

1	2	3	4	5
2	3	3	5	6
1	1	1	1	2
4	4	5	6	7
5	4	4	4	3

1	2	3	4	5
2	3	3	5	6
1	1	1	1	2
4	4	5	6	7
5	4	4	4	3

Fig. 7.2 Max-pooling performed on second row of the matrix with stride rate of 1.

1	2	3	4	5
2	3	3	5	6
1	1	1	1	2
4	4	5	6	7
5	4	4	4	3

Input feature map (5x5)

Max Pooling →

3	3	5	6
3	3	5	6
4	5	6	7
5	5	6	7

Resultant feature map (4x4)

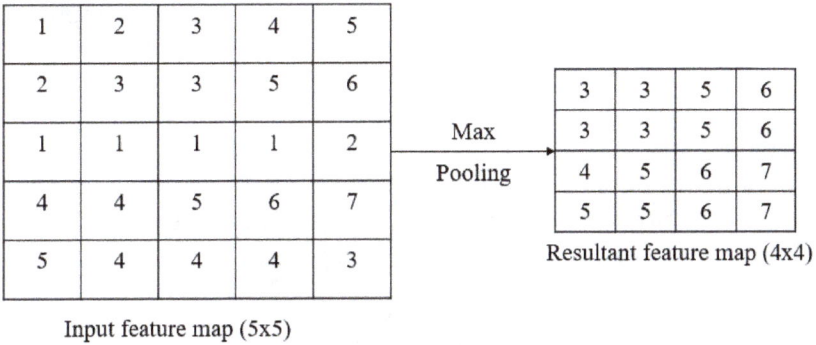

Fig. 7.3 Resultant down-sampled feature map after max-pooling the input feature map.

For stride = 2, the filter slides over input feature map by skipping 2 columns in forward direction after first max-pooling operation. Similarly, moves in downward direction by skipping 2 rows as shown in Fig. 7.4. with filter size is 2x2. However, in this case we fill face the problem of dimension mismatch. Therefore, last column and last row of the input feature map will not be considered in the process of max-pooling.

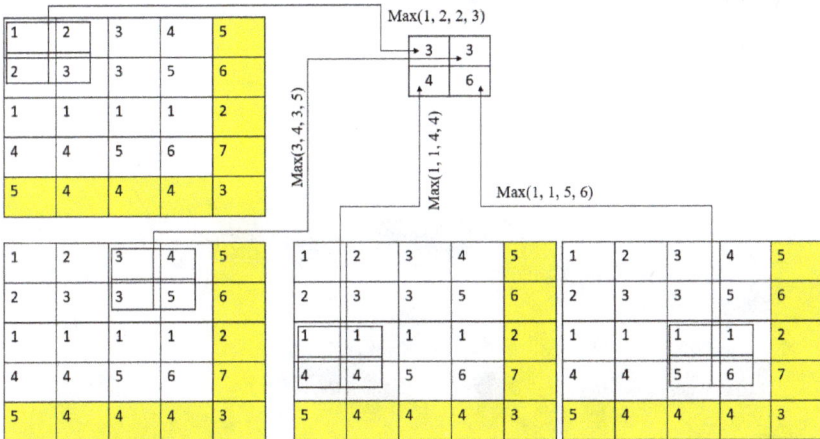

Fig. 7.4 Input feature map of 5x5 and resultant max-pooled feature map of size 2x2. Highlighted row and column will not take part in pooling due to dimension mismatch.

Pooling mainly performed to reduce the dimension of the input matrix. Therefore, use of padding cannot prevent the size reduction of input matrix. However, it can rectify the problem of dimension mismatch during the process of filter convolution over input matrix with particular stride rate. General formula to calculate the required padding shown below in Eq. 1, floor value is taken to avoid the fractional values. The process of convolving filter (f x f) over feature map (n x n) is represented by asterike ('*') symbol.

$$
n \times n * f \times f = floor\left(\frac{n + 2p - f}{s} + 1\right)
$$
$$
\times floor\left(\frac{n + 2p - f}{s} + 1\right) \qquad (1)
$$

Where,
n is the size of input matrix (feature map),
f is size of filter,
p is padding required,
s is stride rate

Now we will see the implementation of max-pooling operation using keras. Example 1, representing the implementation of max-pooling operation.

```
import tensorflow as tf
import numpy as np
```

```
x = np.matrix([[1, 2, 3, 4, 5], [2, 3, 3, 5, 6],
               [1, 1, 1, 1, 2], [4, 4, 5, 6, 7],
               [5, 4, 4, 4, 3]])
```

```
x = x[None, :, :, None]
print(x.shape)
```

```
(1, 5, 5, 1)
```

```
x = tf.keras.layers.MaxPooling2D(pool_size=(2, 2),strides= 1)(x)
```

```
print(x.shape)
```

```
(1, 4, 4, 1)
```

```
print(x[0,:,:,0])
```

```
tf.Tensor(
[[3 3 5 6]
 [3 3 5 6]
 [4 5 6 7]
 [5 5 6 7]], shape=(4, 4), dtype=int32)
```

Example 1. Implementation of max-pooling with pool size/filter 2x2 and stride 1.

In Example 1, a matrix 'x' of size 5x5 taken as input feature map to perform max-pool operation using MaxPooling2D function of keras. As the function accept the input shape of minimum 4 dimension representing the number of feature maps, size of feature map (rows and columns), and number of channels. Therefore, dimensions of input 2D matrix is increased to 4 dimensions before giving it as input to MaxPooling2D function.

x = x[None, :, :, None]

Now the new shape of matrix x is (1, 5, 5, 1) representing single matrix of size 5x5 with one channel. After that, 'x' given as input to Max-Pooling2D function and the resultant matrix with reduced dimension stored back in x.

Now, in example 2, implementation of max-pooling on 'x' with stride rate of 2 is performed.

```python
import tensorflow as tf
import numpy as np
```

```python
x = np.matrix([[1, 2, 3, 4, 5], [2, 3, 3, 5, 6],
               [1, 1, 1, 1, 2], [4, 4, 5, 6, 7],
               [5, 4, 4, 4, 3]])
```

```python
x = x[None, :, :, None]
print(x.shape)
```
```
(1, 5, 5, 1)
```

```python
x = tf.keras.layers.MaxPooling2D(pool_size=(2, 2),strides= 2)(x)
```

```python
print(x.shape)
```
```
(1, 2, 2, 1)
```

```python
print(x[0,:,:,0])
```
```
tf.Tensor(
[[3 5]
 [4 6]], shape=(2, 2), dtype=int32)
```

Example 2. Implementation of max-pooling with stride 2 without padding.

The dimension of resultant feature map in example 2 is down-sampled to the size 2x2 from input feature map of size 5x5. This is because, the last row and column of the input matrix does not participate in max-pooling due to dimension mismatch. As the filter of 2x2 cannot convolve perfectly over an input matrix of size 5x5 with stride of 2. This problem can be solved using padding = 'same' during max-pooling with MaxPooling2D function in keras. Padding in maxpooling never restrict the reduction of size of input matrix. However, it introduce some amount of padding to enable the perfect convolution of filter over input matrix. We can calculate the amount of required padding with the Eq. (1). Let the size of input matrix is 5x5, stride = 2, and filter size = 2 then the required padding will be 0.5 as shown below.

$$floor\left(\frac{5 + 2p - 2}{2} + 1\right) = 3$$

$$p = 0.5$$

In Example 3, we have enabled padding (padding = 'same') which result output feature map of size 3x3 instead of 2x2 as shown in Example 2 without padding (padding = 'valid').

```
import tensorflow as tf
import numpy as np

x = np.matrix([[1, 2, 3, 4, 5], [2, 3, 3, 5, 6],
               [1, 1, 1, 1, 2], [4, 4, 5, 6, 7],
               [5, 4, 4, 4, 3]])

x = x[None, :, :, None]
print(x.shape)

(1, 5, 5, 1)

x = tf.keras.layers.MaxPooling2D(pool_size=(2, 2),strides= 2, padding = 'same')(x)

print(x.shape)

(1, 3, 3, 1)

print(x[0,:,:,0])

tf.Tensor(
[[3 5 6]
 [4 6 7]
 [5 4 3]], shape=(3, 3), dtype=int32)
```

Example 3. Implementation of max-pooling with stride rate = 2 and padding = 'same'.

7.2 Average Pooling

Average pooling is the process of averaging the values of input matrix under the filter patch and create a down-sampled resultant matrix. Visual representation of average pooling of input matrix of size 4x4 using filter of 2x2 shown in Fig. 7.5. The 2x2 filter is convolve over an input matrix from top left corner with stride rate of 1. The average of values of input matrix under filter patch become the first value of the resultant matrix.

1	2	3	4
2	3	3	5
1	1	1	1
4	4	5	6

1	2	3	4
2	3	3	5
1	1	1	1
4	4	5	6

1	2	3	4
2	3	3	5
1	1	1	1
4	4	5	6

Avg(1, 2, 2, 3), Avg(2, 3, 3, 3)
Avg(3, 4, 4, 5)

2	2.75	3.75

1	2	3	4
2	3	3	5
1	1	1	1
4	4	5	6

1	2	3	4
2	3	3	5
1	1	1	1
4	4	5	6

1	2	3	4
2	3	3	5
1	1	1	1
4	4	5	6

Avg(2, 3, 1, 1), Avg(3, 3, 1, 1)
Avg(3, 5, 1, 1)

1.75	2	2.5

1	2	3	4
2	3	3	5
1	1	1	1
4	4	5	6

1	2	3	4
2	3	3	5
1	1	1	1
4	4	5	6

1	2	3	4
2	3	3	5
1	1	1	1
4	4	5	6

Avg(1, 1, 4, 4), Avg(1, 1, 4, 5)
Avg(1, 1, 5, 6)

2.5	2.75	3.25

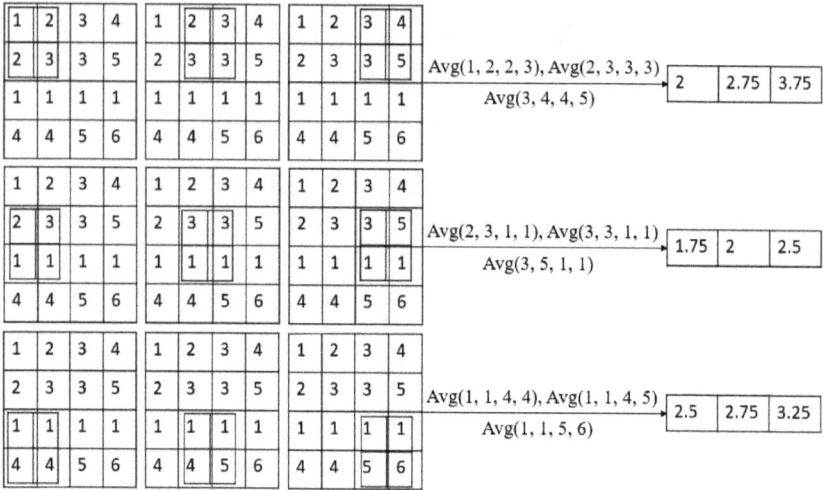

Fig. 7.5 Average pooling with stride = 1.

The implementation of above-average pooling operation with stride rate 1 using AveragePooling2D function of keras shown below in Example 4. In which the input matrix 'x' of size 4x4 is converted into float type, as in case of average pooling the resultant could in fraction also. Therefore, input integer matrix is converted in to float64 using astype() function.

x = x.astype('float64')

Further, the shape of the input matrix 'x' is extended to a valid shape as required by the AveragePooling2D function representing the number of feature maps, size (rows and columns), and number of channels.

x = x[None, :, :, None]

Now the shape of 'x' is extended to 4 dimensions that is (1, 4, 4, 1) representing single matrix with size 4x4 and 1 channel. Further, the 4D matrix is given to AveragePooling2D function as input, which give the down-sampled output of shape (1, 3, 3, 1). The actual resultant matrix displayed on console with print statement.

print(x[0, :, :, 0])

```
import tensorflow as tf
import numpy as np

x = np.matrix([[1, 2, 3, 4], [2, 3, 3, 5],
               [1, 1, 1, 1], [4, 4, 5, 6]])

x = x.astype('float64')

x = x[None, :, :, None]
print(x.shape)

(1, 4, 4, 1)

x = tf.keras.layers.AveragePooling2D(pool_size=(2, 2),
                                     strides= 1,
                                     padding = 'valid')(x)

print(x.shape)

(1, 3, 3, 1)

print(x[0,:,:,0])

tf.Tensor(
[[2.   2.75 3.75]
 [1.75 2.   2.5 ]
 [2.5  2.75 3.25]], shape=(3, 3), dtype=float32)
```

Example 4. Implementation of average pooling with filter size = 2 and stride = 1.

Now, we average pool the input matrix with stride rate of 2 using filter of size 2x2. In case of stride 2, the 2x2 filter convolve over an input matrix starting from top left corner with steps of 2. It means that after calculating the average pool of top-left first 2x2 square of input matrix, we calculate the average pool of next 2x2 square of input matrix. The complete process of average pooling of 4x4 input matrix shown in Fig. 7.6. The first value of the resultant down-sampled 2x2 matrix is calculated by averaging four values (1, 2, 2, 3) of input matrix under 2x2 filter. Average calculated by summing up the values (1+2+2+3 = 8) and dividing it by total values under the filter that is 4. Therefore, we get 2 as first value of resultant 2x2 matrix. Similarly, rest of the values can also be calculated as shown in the figure below.

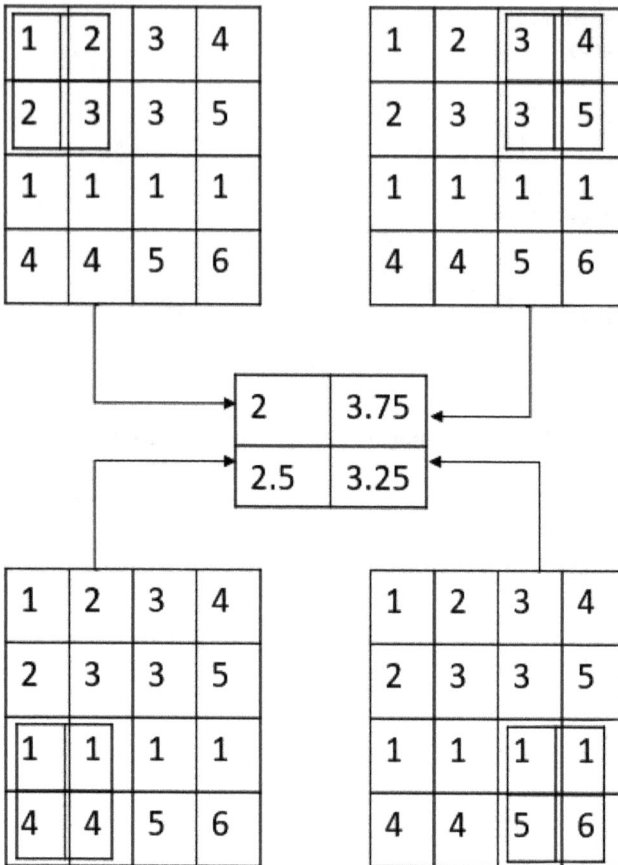

Fig. 7.6 Average pooling of 4x4 matrix with stride rate of 2.

The implementation of above process of average pooling (Fig. 7.6) with stride = 2 and without padding is shown in Example 5. The code mention in Example 5 is almost similar to Example 4, The only difference is the value of stride parameter in AveragePooling2D function of keras. Which is 1 in Example 4 and 2 in Example 5.

```python
import tensorflow as tf
import numpy as np
```

```python
x = np.matrix([[1, 2, 3, 4], [2, 3, 3, 5],
               [1, 1, 1, 1], [4, 4, 5, 6]])
```

```python
x = x.astype('float64')
```

```python
x = x[None, :, :, None]
print(x.shape)
```

```
(1, 4, 4, 1)
```

```python
x = tf.keras.layers.AveragePooling2D(pool_size=(2, 2),
                                     strides= 2,
                                     padding = 'valid')(x)
```

```python
print(x.shape)
```

```
(1, 2, 2, 1)
```

```python
print(x[0,:,:,0])
```

```
tf.Tensor(
[[2.    3.75]
 [2.5  3.25]], shape=(2, 2), dtype=float32)
```

Example 5. Implementation of average pooling with stride = 2 and without padding.

Summary

Pooling is the process of sliding kernels over feature maps to summarize the feature information and reduce dimension. Also, reduce the number of learning parameters and computation time. Moreover, pooling extracts the features irrespective of the feature position. Max-pooling and average-pooling methods are commonly used in deep learning models.

Max pooling, consider the maximum value under each slide of kernel over the input feature-map. Whereas, average pooling calculate the average of all the pixel values under the patch. Sliding of kernel/filter over feature map regulated according to the stride rate. Padding in case of pooling cannot prevent the dimension reduction as in case of convolution. It can rectify the problem of dimension mismatch during pooling process.

Questions

1. What are the advantages of pooling in CNN?
2. Explain max and average pooling with the help of example (stride = 1).
3. *Explain the use of padding in pooling process with the help of an example.
4. *WAP to apply max pooling on color image and display all three pooled feature maps.
5. WAP to apply average pooling on color image and display all the pooled feature maps.
6. Comment on the statement "CNN is independent from the feature position in the input".
7. If max pooling applied on 4x4 matrix using filter of size 2x2 with stride rate of 1, then what will be the size of resultant feature map?
8. What are hyper parameters in pooling layer?
9. Why is it required to down-sample the feature maps?

Solutions:

Question 3

```
import numpy as np
import tensorflow as tf
```

```
x = np.random.randint(100, size = (5,5))
```

```
x = x.astype('float64')
x = x[None, :, :, None]
print(x.shape)
```

```
(1, 5, 5, 1)
```

```
x_nopad = tf.keras.layers.AveragePooling2D(pool_size=(2, 2),
                                           strides= 2,
                                           padding = 'valid')(x)
```

```
print(x_nopad.shape)
```

```
(1, 2, 2, 1)
```

```
x_nopad = tf.keras.layers.AveragePooling2D(pool_size=(2, 2),
                                           strides= 2,
                                           padding = 'valid')(x)
```

```
print(x_nopad.shape)
```

```
(1, 2, 2, 1)
```

```
x_pad = tf.keras.layers.AveragePooling2D(pool_size=(2, 2),
                                         strides= 2,
                                         padding = 'same')(x)
```

```
print(x_pad.shape)
```

```
(1, 3, 3, 1)
```

Question 4

```python
import tensorflow as tf
import matplotlib.image as img
import matplotlib.pyplot as plt
```

```python
img1 = img.imread("lion.jpg")
plt.imshow(img1)
print(img1.shape)
```

(1200, 1600, 3)

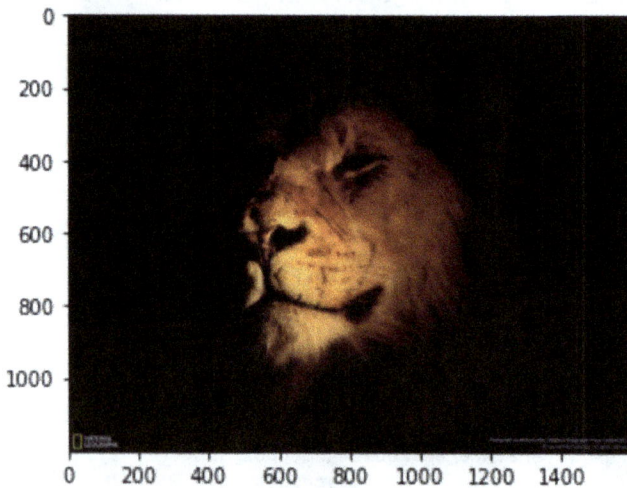

```
print(img1.dtype)
img1 = img1.astype('float64')
print(img1.dtype)
```

```
uint8
float64
```

```
img1 = img1[None, :, :, :]
print(img1.shape)
```

```
(1, 1200, 1600, 3)
```

```
img1 = tf.keras.layers.MaxPooling2D(pool_size=(2, 2),
                                    strides= 1,
                                    padding = 'valid')(img1)
```

```
print(img1.shape)
```

```
(1, 1199, 1599, 3)
```

```
plt.imshow(img1[0,:,:,0])
```

```
<matplotlib.image.AxesImage at 0x24d898790a0>
```

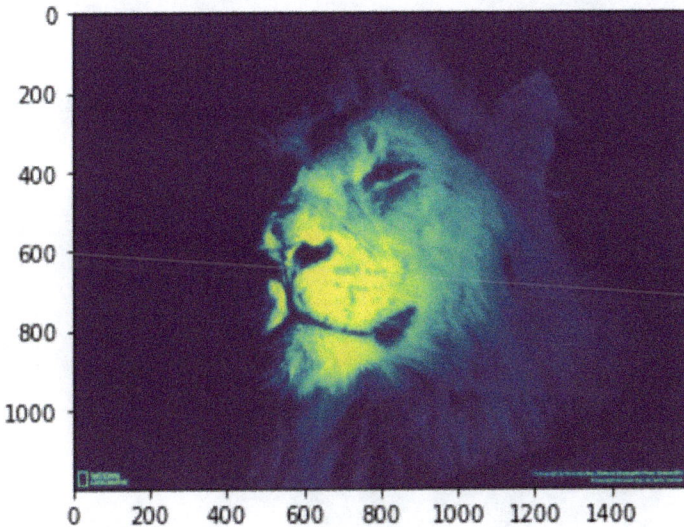

```
plt.imshow(img1[0,:,:,1])
```

`<matplotlib.image.AxesImage at 0x24d898cad30>`

```
plt.imshow(img1[0,:,:,2])
```

```
<matplotlib.image.AxesImage at 0x24d87d336a0>
```

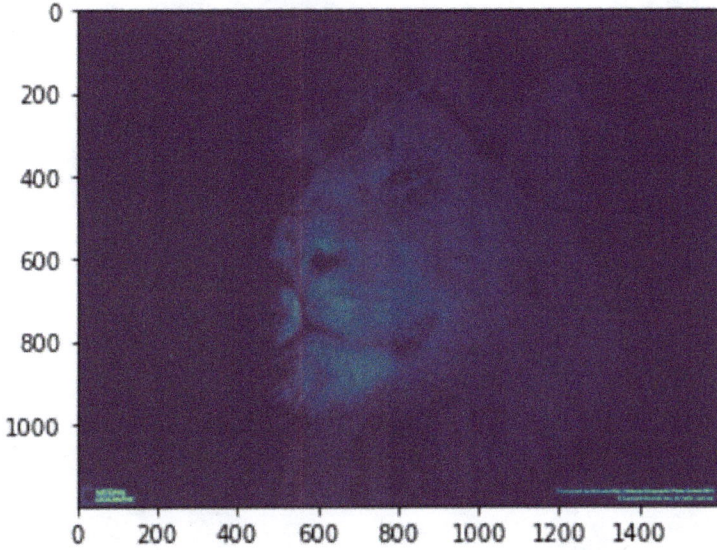

8

Implementation of Convolutional Neural Network in Python

In this chapter, we will implement CNN based model on MNIST (Numeric) dataset ("https://storage.googleapis.com/tensorflow/tf-keras-datasets/"). The dataset consists of pictures of numbers from 0 to 9. The objective of this implementation is to train CNN model to accurately classify the input image of numbers from 0 to 9. The MNIST dataset is having total 70000 images of which 60000 images are used for training purposes and the remaining 10000 for testing.

The following are the supporting libraries required to build the model.

```python
import tensorflow as tf
from keras.preprocessing.image import ImageDataGenerator
from keras.datasets import mnist
import matplotlib.image as img
import matplotlib.pyplot as plt
```

Keras function load_data() extract the MNIST dataset and return the training and testing datasets. These datasets are stored in the variables (trainX, trainY) and (testX, testY). Where trainX, testX are the images of numbers (0 to 9) and trainY, testY are corresponding labels.

```python
(trainX, trainY) , (testX, testY) = mnist.load_data()
```

Let us check the shape of training and testing data to know the exact number of images assigned for training and testing purposes. Which is 60000 for training and 10000 for testing in this case.

```python
print(trainX.shape)
print(testX.shape)

(60000, 28, 28)
(10000, 28, 28)
```

Now we will display some of the sample images from training data with their corresponding labels. These sample images can be displayed together using the function subpot() of matplotlib library. The subplot() function takes three parameters representing the number of row, column, and the index of current plot. And imshow() and title() functions of matplotlib library are used to display the actual image with corresponding title. Further, plt.axis('off') to remove the axes in the images and to create more white spaces between the images.

```python
for i in range(6):
    ax = plt.subplot(2, 3, i+1)
    plt.imshow(trainX[i])
    plt.title(trainY[i])
    plt.axis("off")
```

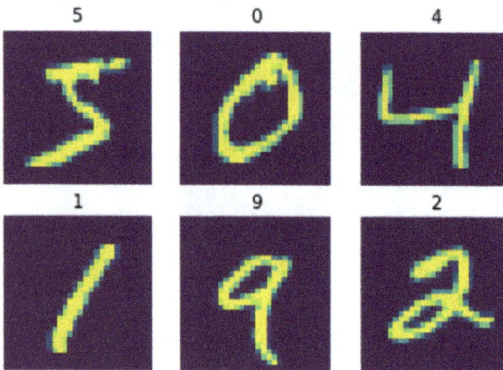

As the MNIST dataset is already very much processed and very good dataset, therefore not much data pre-processing will be required. Here, we reshape the images to add one more dimension representing the number of channels (1 in this case). Further, normalize the data within the range of 0 to 1. Before normalization, both training and testing data converted from int to float. As, 255 is the maximum pixel value for any grey scale image. Therefore, normalization is carried out by dividing every pixel of all images by 255.

```python
trainX = trainX.reshape((trainX.shape[0], 28, 28, 1))
testX = testX.reshape((testX.shape[0], 28, 28, 1))
```

```python
print(trainX.shape)
```

```
(60000, 28, 28, 1)
```

```
trainX = trainX.astype('float32')
testX = testX.astype('float32')
trainX = trainX / 255.0
testX = testX / 255.0
```

As the MNIST dataset is having 10 classes (images of numbers from 0 to 9). Therefore, we convert the trainY and testY (vectors) into the binary matrix using to_categorial() function of keras library. Each value of the vectors is represented by the binary number of length 10. For example, if the number is 5 then it will be represented binary number of lengths 10 with 9 zeros and 1 one. Further, one will be placed at position 5 starting from index 0 that is [0 0 0 0 0 1 0 0 0 0].

```
for i in range(5):
    print(trainY[i])
```

```
5
0
4
1
9
```

```
from keras.utils import np_utils
trainY = np_utils.to_categorical(trainY, 10)
testY = np_utils.to_categorical(testY, 10)
```

```
print(trainY)
```

```
[[0. 0. 0. ... 0. 0. 0.]
 [1. 0. 0. ... 0. 0. 0.]
 [0. 0. 0. ... 0. 0. 0.]
 ...
 [0. 0. 0. ... 0. 0. 0.]
 [0. 0. 0. ... 0. 0. 0.]
 [0. 0. 0. ... 0. 1. 0.]]
```

Now, using keras API we build a convolutional neural network model. Sequential class is used to linearly stack the layers of the model. Add() method is used for adding layers in the model (cnn in this case). The model is having total seven layers with an output layer having 10 units (nodes) each representing separate class of data (numbers from 0 to 9). In addition, as the dataset is having more than 2 classes therefore, softmax activation function in used instead of sigmoid. Model is having two convolutional layer with activation function ReLU and 32 filters each of size 3x3. Further, model is having two maxpooling layers with window size of 2x2 and stride rate of 2.

```
cnn = tf.keras.models.Sequential()

cnn.add(tf.keras.layers.Conv2D(filters=32, kernel_size=3,
                               activation='relu',
                               input_shape=[28, 28, 1]))

cnn.add(tf.keras.layers.MaxPool2D(pool_size=2, strides=2))

cnn.add(tf.keras.layers.Conv2D(filters=32, kernel_size=3,
                               activation='relu'))

cnn.add(tf.keras.layers.MaxPool2D(pool_size=2, strides=2))

cnn.add(tf.keras.layers.Flatten())

cnn.add(tf.keras.layers.Dense(units=128, activation='relu'))

cnn.add(tf.keras.layers.Dense(units=10, activation='softmax'))
```

The compile() function is used to configure the model before training. In which, 'adam' optimizer is used for adjusting the weights of the model. For computing loss, 'catagorial_crossentropy' is used. In addition, 'accuracy' metric used for analyze the performance of the model.

```
cnn.compile(optimizer = 'adam',
            loss = 'categorical_crossentropy',
            metrics = ['accuracy'])
```

Now, we train the model (cnn) using fit() function with batch size of 128 and for 25 epochs. Where, batch size means the training data is divided into multiple batches of particular size. Moreover, an epoch means the passing of all the data through the network and weights are adjusted accordingly. To show the training progress and one epoch per line we use verbose=1. Further, (testX, testY) data used to analyze the performance of the model.

```
batch_size = 128
num_epoch = 25
history = cnn.fit(trainX, trainY,
                  batch_size=batch_size,
                  epochs=num_epoch, verbose=1,
                  validation_data=(testX, testY))
```

```
Epoch 1/25
469/469 [==============================] - 19s 41ms/step - loss: 0.2481 - accuracy: 0.9290
0.9761
Epoch 2/25
469/469 [==============================] - 18s 39ms/step - loss: 0.0646 - accuracy: 0.9806
0.9829
Epoch 3/25
469/469 [==============================] - 18s 38ms/step - loss: 0.0457 - accuracy: 0.9858
0.9843
Epoch 4/25
469/469 [==============================] - 18s 38ms/step - loss: 0.0348 - accuracy: 0.9894
0.9896
Epoch 5/25
469/469 [==============================] - 18s 38ms/step - loss: 0.0274 - accuracy: 0.9915
0.9891
Epoch 6/25
469/469 [==============================] - 18s 39ms/step - loss: 0.0218 - accuracy: 0.9933
0.9902
```

We can use summary() method to check the total number of parameters used in training of the model.

```
cnn.summary()
```

Model: "sequential_2"

Layer (type)	Output Shape	Param #
conv2d_4 (Conv2D)	(None, 26, 26, 32)	320
max_pooling2d_4 (MaxPooling 2D)	(None, 13, 13, 32)	0
conv2d_5 (Conv2D)	(None, 11, 11, 32)	9248
max_pooling2d_5 (MaxPooling 2D)	(None, 5, 5, 32)	0
flatten_2 (Flatten)	(None, 800)	0
dense_4 (Dense)	(None, 128)	102528
dense_5 (Dense)	(None, 10)	1290

```
Total params: 113,386
Trainable params: 113,386
Non-trainable params: 0
```

Now the model is evaluated over test dataset using evaluate() method of tensorflow library. The function return the loss and accuracy of test dataset.

```
score = cnn.evaluate(testX, testY)
print('Test loss:', score[0])
print('Test accuracy:', score[1])
```

```
313/313 [==============================] - 1s 3ms/step - loss: 0.0427 - accuracy: 0.9914
Test loss: 0.04269498214125633
Test accuracy: 0.9914000034332275
```

The performance of the model can also be represented by plotting the loss and accuracy curve for each epoch during training of the model. With the help of history attribute of keras library. History attribute is a record of accuracy and loss as per each epoch during the process of training for both training and validation data.

```
plt.plot(history.history['accuracy'])
plt.plot(history.history['val_accuracy'])
plt.title('model accuracy')
plt.ylabel('accuracy')
plt.xlabel('epoch')
plt.legend(['Train', 'Validation'], loc='upper left')
plt.show()
```

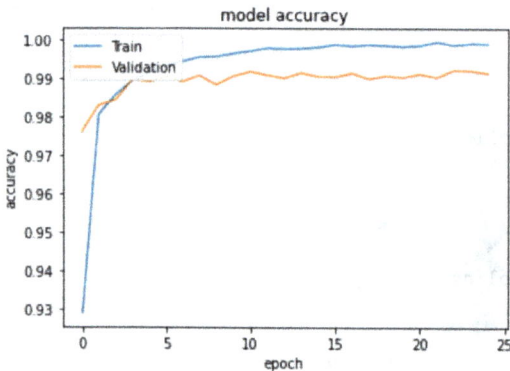

Similarly, we can plot the graph for training and validation loss.

```
plt.plot(history.history['loss'])
plt.plot(history.history['val_loss'])
plt.title('model loss')
plt.ylabel('loss')
plt.xlabel('epoch')
plt.legend(['Train', 'Validation'], loc='upper left')
plt.show()
```

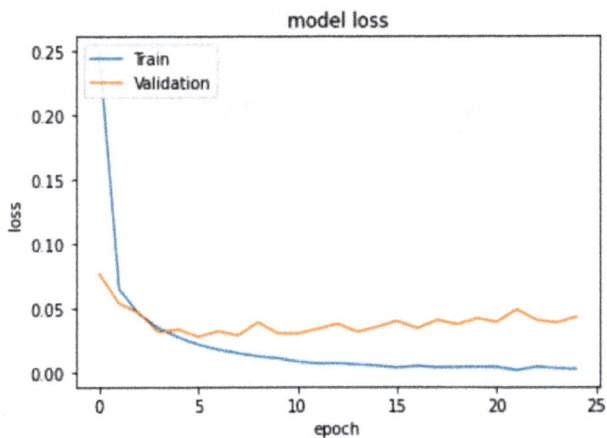

www.ingramcontent.com/pod-product-compliance
Lightning Source LLC
Chambersburg PA
CBHW071704210326
41597CB00017B/2329